CHANGE YOUR LIFE!

POWERFUL TOOLS FOR LIFE CHANGING RESULTS

David Fox

BALBOA.
PRESS

A DIVISION OF HAY HOUSE

Balboa Press books may be ordered through booksellers or by contacting:

Balboa Press
A Division of Hay House
1663 Liberty Drive
Bloomington, IN 47403
www.balboapress.com
1-(877) 407-4847

ISBN: 978-1-4525-3265-3 (sc)
ISBN: 978-1-4525-3268-4 (hc)
ISBN: 978-1-4525-3267-7 (e)

Library of Congress Control Number: 2011902154

Printed in the United States of America

Balboa Press rev. date: 9/10/2012

To my boys Jake and Brandon, love you forever

CONTENTS

INTRODUCTION

Have you ever wondered where your moods come from? Have you ever wished that you had absolute control over how you feel, your level of motivation, your ability to handle stress and anxiety and to create the things you want in your life? Well, then you have come to the right place. This book was written with the sole purpose of helping you learn how to master your thoughts, beliefs, and emotions and consequently how to achieve what you want out of your life. This is also a book about change. In all its forms, change is a major factor in life that we all have to deal with. Whether it's change that we want to create for ourselves or change that life forces upon us, we need to know how to effectively manage change in our lives and how to actively create and maintain the changes that we desire.

It is only through such mastery that you can create lasting and significant success in your life as well as help others around you to achieve the same. It's all about *changing your mind* and deciding that you will no longer be ruled by the seemingly uncontrollable events, people, thoughts, feelings and moods that plague you, to a greater or lesser extent, on a daily basis. It is about getting yourself out of disempowering states and also being able to withstand the moods and negative thoughts of the people around you.

This book is about making your own parade, even in the rain, and going forward in your life with confidence and a feeling of peacefulness and, of course, with a big smile on your face!

There are many books written on positive thinking, some are religious in nature and others more scientific in their approach. I feel that by looking at only one area or approach to self-help, one may be shutting oneself off from the very technique, tool, or strategy that could help you achieve what you want. We will focus on a number of different and versatile ways that you could achieve your desired outcome — such as the essential nature of your thoughts and how they relate directly to your moods, your emotional states and thus the actions that you take towards the fulfilment of your dreams and goals. It's about changing your mind towards an orientation to success, health, happiness, abundance, and peace of mind.

You will be taken on a journey into your mind to understand why *you* are ultimately responsible for your moods, your actions, and thus your level of satisfaction with your life and the success you have achieved so far. You will learn that it is really you who decides your own reality and who has the choice of how to interpret the circumstances and events in your life.

You will see from this book that blaming the outside world for your experience in life is a fruitless exercise because you will come to *know* that it is your inner world that you must change in order to change anything in your outer world. That goes for your relationships, your body, your financial status, your success, and, of course your contentment and happiness with your life. This book will show you how to get yourself out of negative states and into positive states that are lasting and real. It will show you that you don't need drugs (illegal ones that is!), alcohol, or any other artificial mood enhancers to feel good about yourself and the world.

You could think of this book as a "hitchhiker's guide to your mind." Each chapter and topic is like a different tool that you can reach for whenever you feel stuck or need some reminding of what you can do to help move yourself forward again in your life.

I don't pretend that everything you will read in this book will be new to you. If you are reading this book, you probably have read others that are similar (but not the same!) and will have come across some of these ideas before. However, it is my sincere hope that this will be the time it clicks for you or makes sense in a way that gets you to take action and start using these ideas to help you in your own life as it has helped my clients, friends, family, and myself.

This book draws on many of the same principles that have been put forward by some of the greatest thinkers in psychology, in mind power, positive thought, and life changing strategies that really work. It also reflects on my own experiences with these ideas as well as the experiences of the people I have counselled in using these techniques to make positive changes in their lives. As such, this is not by any means a book of theory but a book of practical and time tested techniques that anyone can use.

I have used the tools and techniques outlined in this book to rid myself of generalized anxiety, to help create abundance, to find a partner for life and to achieve many other personal and professional goals that often seemed as remote to me as a dream. I have learned how to make them real and how to let go and enjoy the process along the way. I continue to use the techniques today and I continue to help others do the same. It is my sincere wish that you will find that they work just as well for you — as I believe they will — and that you learn that change is not as hard as you once thought and that it can be very rewarding and exciting.

I invite you to join me on this journey of discovery and see if what I am saying here is true or not. I dare you to try the suggestions that I make. I don't ever claim to speak the absolute truth, what I do say is that these are the principles that I have found that seem to be working in our universe and I would invite you to try them and see if you agree. I would love to hear from you once you have given it a go. I am open to suggestions! But like I said, I have tried them, I know they work if you persist, use them consistently, and make sure you stay disciplined to what they have to offer.

You can change your mind! All you have to do is the preparation for that point when you decide you will no longer be ruled by negative thoughts, emotions, and mediocrity and claim your right to live your life the way you want.

Welcome to my book. I really hope you enjoy it and most of all that it leads you to where you want to be in life.

David Fox
david@foxpsychology.com.au

CHAPTER 1 — POSITIVE THINKING

The Pop Psychology that Works

The concept of using positive thinking to help improve one's life circumstances has been around a very long time, but it was Dr. Norman Vincent Peale who coined the phrase "positive thinking" in the 1950s with his book *The Power of Positive Thinking*. Since then, many books have been written on the subject and, in psychology, the new field of cognitive-behavioural psychology began to take shape in the 1950s as a response to a growing desire to bring psychology into mainstream sciences and move away from the purely psychodynamic world of Sigmund Freud and Carl Jung. It was Dr. Albert Ellis and later Dr. Aaron T. Beck in the 1960s who developed this new school of psychology and who started having great success with patients by helping them with their thoughts and behavior. I doubt very much that Dr. Peale, who wrote his book in the early 1950s, was aware that many of the principles he mentioned in his book were closely related to the concepts that were growing in academic and professional psychology and which have now become entrenched and well regarded as a form of therapy very well suited to the treatment of anxiety and depressive disorders.

There is indeed, a power in positive "rational" thinking that when utilized to its fullest potential can transform your life from anxiety,

1

low self-esteem, and unhappiness into strength, confidence, and joy. I have seen time and again how faulty thinking patterns lead people to feel miserable and anxious when in reality, there is truly nothing for them to be upset about. In fact, they seem to have achieved so much and have so much evidence that they are resourceful and competent but they resolutely refuse to see this. They seem to be making a conscious or subconscious "choice" to filter out the good in their lives. I put the word choice in quotation marks because, as you will see later on, our thinking can become so automatic that we don't even make a conscious choice about what to think and what to believe.

Positive thinking or "thought work" as I like to call it, is not a some-time thing, it is an all-time thing. If you do not work on it constantly, always catching yourself when you are thinking negatively or irrationally and then deliberately thinking or voicing something positive, then it is unlikely that it will have the desired effect. However, if you learn the techniques in this book and constantly apply them to your life, you will see some major changes in how you start to feel and the results you are getting. One of the hardest things to do is to be able to maintain a positive state of mind on a constant basis. Obviously no one is ever always up or always down, but what one tries to achieve is to stay above that imaginary line that would divide the two extremes. In other words, we all want to be a little bit optimistic rather than a little bit depressed or anxious; a little bit happy rather than a little bit sad

As an example, there have been days in my life where I would be going about my business and for seemingly no reason at all I might start experiencing powerful feelings of negativity and doubt (I have since then been experiencing these seemingly uncontrollable negative moods less and less as I have practiced the strategies that I will mention in this book). What did I doubt? Everything! I would feel as if everything in the world was wrong. These intensely powerful feelings and emotions would often cloud my reasoning and inevitably lead to more negative thoughts, which would then perpetuate the whole cycle of negative emotions leading to further negative thoughts, disempowering beliefs and behaviors. Is this ringing a bell for you?

When I first began to study the concept of positive thinking, I worked purely with affirmations or "thought replacement." What

I was able to do with increasing effectiveness was to change these negative feelings into positive ones through the use of encouraging and positive affirmations. There are many other great books written about the power of affirmations and I am sure you have come across a few good ones yourself. The way I went about using these affirmations was to immediately start to either voice positive statements or to get myself to think positively. An important fact that I would like to make here is that I often did not believe the positive statements that I made. The reason for this is because I was feeling so bad at that moment that I couldn't see any way that the positive things I was saying were actually true. There is a specific method I will show you later on that will take you through the steps of changing your thoughts in a similar fashion, even though you won't *feel* at first what you have written down as an alternative is true or valid.

What I began to notice, however, was that whether I believed the statements that I made or not was usually irrelevant to the *outcome*, which was that after a period of time my mood started to lift and I started seeing things in a more positive (rational) light. It is really amazing when you learn to be the master of your thoughts and therefore your emotions how your whole outlook on life can change. After a period of time, when you think back to the time when you didn't feel in control, you can hardly believe you are the same person. You will think: "Was that me? Did I really think like that? Did I really believe that?" I am excited because you have chosen to follow this path by choosing to read this book.

One of the problems that I found in my struggle to keep a positive frame of mind is that once I had achieved that state that is above the imaginary line between being unhappy and happy, I often let it slip away. How did I let it slip away? I mistakenly believed that I would continue to feel positive even if I did not continue to use the techniques. What eventually happens is that without that conscious effort to keep your mind in shape, the negative thoughts start working their way back in. Negative thoughts are sly, they have a way of building themselves up in your mind slowly like a fungus, until they have built themselves up into a formidable force that often seems hard if not impossible to eliminate. So what is the solution for those who are struggling with the process of maintaining a positive mental attitude? Keep at it!

If you plant a seed in the ground and water it every day, it starts to grow towards the surface. If you don't know and trust that this seed is growing, you will doubt whether anything at all is happening *underneath the surface*. You may start to say: "I don't believe in this! I water this piece of ground every day but I never see any results for all my hard work!" Part of life is trusting that if you put in the effort, the outcome is already happening with your very intention and then your action. Eventually, one day, that little plant breaks through the soil with its green, new stem. And from there, you watch it grow stronger and more vital every day (*as long as you keep looking after it and watering it!*).

Like I said, negative thoughts are sly, they are often perpetuated by your subconscious in that they can become so automatic that you might never notice that you are actually thinking negatively. The first big step that anyone must make if they truly want to stop the negativity, become more positive and change their lives is to *recognise those negative automatic thoughts as they appear.* You must start to catch your thoughts. This is a big step towards the eventual elimination of those negative thoughts because it is only once we recognise where the problems lie that we can take action to correct them.

The following chapters are various reflections on how you can go about changing your life through conscious and subconscious control of your mind and body. The chapters also include various reflections on life issues that we all have to deal with. The issues that are dealt with are looked at in a way that I hope will be helpful to you on your journey. I hope that by consistently applying the practical suggestions that are made, you will be able to live a more fulfilling, more productive and less stressful life and that you will truly be able to change your mind about life, what it holds for you, and the heights you can reach if you just try.

CHAPTER 2 — WHAT IS YOUR MIND AND HOW DO YOU CHANGE IT?

When we speak about the mind, we are referring to something that seems to have eluded complete understanding by everyone from poets to neuroscientists even to this day. What is a mind? What does it consist of? Is it your brain alone with its neurons and synapses transmitting signals all day long or is it something more? Surely there is more to us as human beings who think, feel, laugh, cry, and play than the gray matter that sits between our ears?

We know that there are two very different parts of our minds, which we call our conscious and sub-conscious minds. Who we are in our waking reality is derived mostly from our conscious mind, but this in turn is influenced by our subconscious mind, which is a powerful force that we can use either for us or against us. This is an essential point that you must understand. Your subconscious is like electricity, if not controlled and used for constructive purposes, it can be extremely dangerous and even deadly to you. It can lift you up to levels of happiness and fulfilment that you could never have imagined or it can strike you down into the lowest levels of despair. The choice is yours. Let's learn a bit about the subconscious and see if we can understand what it is and how we can use it as a great ally in life.

The Subconscious Mind

Many years ago, Dr. Joseph Murphy wrote a book entitled *The Power of Your Subconscious Mind*,[1] which details the incredible power that our subconscious has to influence our lives and shows how we can use this to help us reach just about any important and realistic goal in life. However, it can also become filled with negative beliefs that could destroy our lives if we let just any thoughts be "planted" in its fertile soil. You see, your subconscious mind, which is below the level of conscious everyday thinking, does not distinguish between right and wrong or what is a valid command or not. The subconscious will act on whatever thoughts you consistently repeat to it and will begin influencing your beliefs and therefore your behaviors and the outcomes you see happening in your life. It is the same concept with your body: it will only give you what you put into it. If you feed it garbage it will not work powerfully to do your bidding. However if you feed it nourishing, healthy food it will give you power, health, vitality, and happiness. You might like to think of the mind as an iceberg — your conscious mind is the tip that protrudes above the water and your subconscious is the rest of your mind that lies beneath the surface of your everyday life. Although you may not see the operation of the subconscious mind, it is always there, subtly influencing you and it does have the power to radically affect your emotions and the achievement of your goals in life.

As an example, I counseled a young lady a few years ago who was an ex-drug addict. She had turned to drugs as a way of dealing with the seemingly uncontrollable and ghastly events that had happened to her in the course of her life. She was a very friendly and likeable woman who just seemed to have had a lot of tough breaks. As counselling progressed, I could tell from the sentences she used to describe herself and her life that she had some seriously limiting beliefs about herself and that she was reinforcing them every day as she let the thoughts come and go in her mind without scrutinizing whether they were in fact rational or true. As we got further into counselling, I discovered a life event that had played a major role in influencing her belief system and subconscious mind.

[1] Murphy, Dr.J. (1963). The Power of your Subconscious Mind. New Jersey: Prentice Hall.

When she was 16, she had been sent by her parents to a center that supposedly helped young kids get over a drug habit by using religious instruction and "education." She told me that the school had actively and consistently told her that the reason she had had such negative experiences in her life was because she was a bad person and that every time something negative or bad happened to her (or anyone else in her family) it was because she had done something bad to cause it. Thus, when her mother hurt herself, it was her fault for being a bad daughter. When she was hijacked and almost raped, it was her fault because of something she had done before. Although the people at the clinic may have helped her dry out from her drug habit, they actually just replaced her drug habit with a potentially even more dangerous and destructive habit — a subconscious belief system that blamed her for everything bad that ever happened to her. When I asked whether she believed that the good things that happened to her were her own doing, she said that good things were just lucky events and had nothing to do with her. She didn't or couldn't create them. This is fairly common and known in the field of psychology as false attribution theory. Essentially it's when people blame themselves for many if not all of the negative events that occur in their lives and refuse to take responsibility for the good that happens, saying they were just lucky or it was a coincidence. How disempowering!

I knew that the first step was to begin to show her and help her discover these faulty and harmful beliefs. I got her to start catching her thoughts every time something happened to her, write them down, and bring them to our sessions. We identified from those thoughts her belief system and what she really believed about herself and life in her subconscious mind. I then went on, when I felt she was ready, to explain to her that it was these beliefs and ideas that were actually helping to bring about the very negative things that she was trying to avoid and which were causing her such pain and misery. When she started to see and understand how her thoughts and beliefs were working against her and how negatively loaded her subconscious mind was, she began to make progress. She started seeing things differently and thus began to handle situations in her life and view events in a much more rational and realistic way. She started to recover from despising herself and from her terribly low self-esteem. In time she was able to see that some events happen just randomly and that there was no way she could hold herself responsible for something like someone stealing her cell phone in a shopping center and she also started to appreciate her own bravery in dealing with her difficult life and to feel a bit more empowered.

As you can see from the above example, your subconscious mind works on belief systems that are instilled in it from the time you are born and may have been put there by parents, siblings, teachers, friends, or anything and anyone who had an influence on you, good or bad. It is up to you to start challenging your own beliefs and thoughts, and you do this by starting to notice which areas of your life you may be having difficulty with or which don't seem to be working for you. You then start to monitor your thoughts and feelings (especially when you feel negative and down) to start to look for the triggers that cause you to feel bad. Once you find the exact point at which you started to feel bad, you need to remember what you were thinking and feeling at the time and start to write those thoughts down in a thought journal.

One of the biggest problems with our upbringing creating negative and faulty beliefs in us, is not that it happened, but that we don't recognise that it happened or try to change these beliefs. In fact, most of the time we keep on reinforcing them long after the original beliefs were planted instead of rooting them out and throwing them away!

In recognizing how you have been affected by your past, you must use this knowledge to your advantage. If you want to use it to blame those around you because of what they did to you or the ideas and beliefs they gave you, you are only disempowering yourself and creating resentment and anger in your mind and body. You don't need those in your life. Use the information to help you discover who you are today so that you can understand why you are the way you are and then go right ahead and change your mind! Let's look a bit deeper at what beliefs are.

Beliefs

Your beliefs are made up of what I would call *surface beliefs* and *core beliefs*.

Your surface beliefs are the ones that are derived from a number of thoughts that usually link to any number of more essential, core beliefs. For example, my surface belief that I am good at math may be based on the thoughts I have about how I did on my exam, but if I were to take that to the next level of a core belief, it would be the belief that I am an intelligent person. That is a core belief, which could have been entrenched from any number of sources, for example, from the time you first tied your shoes laces and were told how clever and intelligent you were or when you got your first A on a test at school.

It is your core beliefs that most dramatically affect your thoughts, emotions, behaviors, and thus ultimately your life as a whole. It is the negative core beliefs that you will need to work with as we go through this book showing you how to extract them and the thoughts that give them fuel, and rid yourself of them, or at least with your new awareness keep them under control. In addition to this, we will also be working to instil new, positive, and rational beliefs to replace the old, negative ones. In changing your beliefs, which are the major content of your subconscious mind, you will learn to change your mind and your life forever.

The key to living your life the way you want, then, is to take this powerful tool, your subconscious mind, and make sure that it is working for you and that you create positive, rational beliefs that empower you to move forward and grow. This process begins with finding out what your existing beliefs about yourself and your life already are and then examining whether they are rational, supportive, and true. Once you have done that, you can then replace them with positive, rational beliefs, as the mind abhors a vacuum. Don't just pull the weeds out, but plant and cultivate a whole new garden of flowers!

There are many ways that you can access your current belief systems. One of them is to start to be very aware of your life conditions right now and what your current experience of life is.

This is because your outer life is a mirrored reflection of what you believe and think about every day. My suggestion then is for you to start a *thought journal*, which would begin to get you to see what you think and then start to look deeper into those thoughts and see recurring patterns or themes that you can then put together under a heading. The more thoughts you have about a particular topic, the more likely that, firstly it is a subject that you need to focus on, and secondly, that it is possibly one of your core beliefs.

If you look at Appendix 1, at the end of the book, you will find a journal I have created that you can copy and use to do this activity. I suggest you keep the journal near to you, possibly in a diary, briefcase, or organizer. That way you can be near it and jot down thoughts that disturb you or intrigue you immediately.

At the end of each week, examine your journal of thoughts and make circles around the thoughts that are similar or are based on the same topic or subject. Review what you have written down about what you think the beliefs are behind the thoughts and what you have committed to doing to start to change these to be more supporting for you.

To find your core beliefs, you would need to look at those surface beliefs and try and see what they are telling you about a deep-rooted belief that you have about yourself and the people and world around you.

Please remember that core and surface beliefs are either good for you or bad for you depending on whether they empower you or disempower you. You will usually be able to detect the disempowering beliefs quite easily as they are the ones that make you feel *lousy, depressed or anxious!*

These are the ones we would like to examine, bring out into the light to expose them for the fraudsters they are, and then replace them with your newly designed and improved thoughts and belief systems.

When you begin to establish what your core beliefs are, you will start to notice times when you have what seems like a revelation, where you remember events and situations from your past, or people who influenced you, which created those core beliefs. You will begin to see where many of your disempowering characteristics come from and this is an excellent beginning to changing your beliefs. You can believe anything you want, it makes no difference to your subconscious mind, but it will make a huge difference to the conditions of your life, including how you feel, where you get to with regards to your dreams and goals, and how you experience your life every day.

How do you now start to create new beliefs and influence your subconscious mind?

You use affirmations, meditation, thought replacement, writing out your new goals and your new beliefs and affirming them every day, and you do all this by using the conscious mind!

However, before we go into a discussion on your conscious mind, I'd like to tell you a little bit about hypnosis.

Hypnosis: the superhighway to your subconscious mind!

If you are interested in a way to affect your subconscious mind directly, without having to go through the conscious mind, you could start to learn about hypnosis. Hypnosis, as a practice. has been going on for centuries. Its effectiveness has been well documented and researched. From a surgeon who proved that she could self-hypnotise herself not to bleed when she cut herself, to miraculous physical recoveries of some of the most dreaded diseases, there is no doubt that hypnosis is a very powerful tool for change. Being as powerful as it is, clinical hypnosis should never be used by an untrained person. An untrained person could potentially leave damaging suggestions in another person's subconscious mind or get involved in a situation with a client they don't know how to resolve effectively, leaving the client possibly worse off than before.

However, the reason that it can be so effective is that when you are under hypnosis your conscious mind is much more relaxed and lets its guard down. Your ego has less of a chance to get in the way and your real feelings, thoughts, and beliefs about anything in your life can be revealed. It also allows you to influence your subconscious mind directly with new thoughts, beliefs, and ideas without your conscious mind jumping in and saying, "Hey! That's not true, you really are lousy at math, what about that time you failed a math test in Grade 2?" So, by using hypnosis you are more relaxed, your mind does not resist the new suggestions and they are given freely over to your subconscious, which will eventually accept anything you tell it is true.

If you already know that you have some limiting core beliefs and you would like to change them, you can learn to do self-hypnosis. However, if you really want to get the best results, it may be useful to look into using a professionally trained psychologist who has been trained in clinical hypnosis. While I will not be going into the "how-tos" of self-hypnosis (you can find many excellent books on the subject), I will go through some similar techniques that will allow you to work with the subconscious mind more directly later on in the book.

The Conscious Mind

Your conscious mind is the part of you that you use every day to think, feel, consider, reflect, and imagine. It is like the central processing unit of a computer, which receives all types of information from your senses and your brain through your thoughts and then has to make sense of all of these stimuli so that you can function. It analyzes, compares, and compartmentalizes things for you without your having to do much at all to help.

The conscious mind is the tool that you use to access and influence the subconscious mind when you want to work consciously to change. It is the tool that gives you the ability to scrutinize your thoughts and thus your beliefs and to expose them so that you are then free to see whether these thoughts and beliefs are rational and realistic using the tools that I will give you later on in the book. You will find as you become more adept at using the techniques from cognitive-behavioural therapy that just about any time you are feeling anxious, afraid, stressed, or fearful, you have been thinking limiting and irrational thoughts, which are drawn from your negative and usually false beliefs.

What Are Thoughts?

Are thoughts things? Do they have a basis in physical reality or are they pure energy? Is a thought a firing of a neuron in your brain and the link or tons of links that it makes with other neurons?

Neuropsychologists study the brain and how it functions and they know that if certain areas of your brain get damaged, you will not "think" in a way that is rational or even functional. So there is a basis for saying that your level of thinking is directly related to the level of functioning that your brain has. As long as you are a normal, healthy individual, you will be able to construct, link, and control the thoughts in your head. There are also a number of different ways in which we organize our thoughts. Without methods of screening, associating, and grouping our thoughts, we would have too much information to deal with every day to be able to function effectively. We thus use systems such as *mental filters* to make sense of all the information coming at us internally and externally. We assimilate information so that once we have encountered something we don't have to make sense of it again the next time. This is all part of learning. Sometimes we use and rely on these systems too much, such as when we meet a new person and just from the look of them we immediately put them into a previous grouping of people. This is stereotyping, and people do it all the time before they actually find out who and what that person is all about. They are basically saying: "I don't need any more information about this person because I know who they are and what they are about." We do this because it's easier than having to get to know that person and create new distinctions for our brains to use! This illustrates to you that there are certain systems in your brain that will take information and automatically do something with it, sometimes before you get a chance to consciously review it. The message that I want to get across to you, which is the underlying message in this book, is that you can wake up from this "mind sleep" and start to use your conscious and subconscious minds to your advantage by creating new distinctions, new associations, and new methods of dealing with the world around you.

We could debate the issue of what a thought actually is, but the most important thing to remember about thoughts is that they come from you. You are the one thinking every thought that crosses your mind. It may seem like thoughts appear out of the blue, but YOU are the thinker of your thoughts and it is you who determines which thoughts you would like to have and thus the beliefs that you will use to run your life. Sometimes when we feel like thoughts have just popped into our heads from seemingly nowhere at all, it is possible that your subconscious is sending you a message about something it is working through.

Your conscious mind is the tool that you must use to entrench in yourself the thoughts and beliefs that will empower you and bring you the success and happiness that you want.

You have the power over your thoughts. Any time you are experiencing a number of thoughts, it is up to you to stop them if they are negative or distressing. There is a technique called "thought-stopping" where you catch a thought dead in its tracks and "squash" it before it links to a similar negative or disempowering thought. There are various ways in which you can change these thoughts or stop them.

Quick Tips to Manage a Distressed Mind

1. Picturing the thought

Visualise a particular thought as an object in your mind. For example, if you are anxious, picture a cold, scared, and shivering puppy, and then imagine that you take that puppy and with magic you make it grow bigger, stronger, and more confident until it is a fully grown, powerful animal. Imagine that you and your thoughts are being transformed in the same way.

2. Imagine your mind as a lake

At the point where you feel thoughts are rushing at you and you cannot control them, start to picture your mind as a lake that is experiencing rough conditions with very choppy waves and plenty of swells, imagine that it is also dark overhead and stormy. Now, start to change the scenery in your mind. The clouds start to move away, the sun comes out and you can feel the warmth. The lake water starts to settle down and the waves get smaller and smaller until they are just small swells (these are your thoughts). The swells get smaller and smaller until the water surface becomes still and clear. All is peaceful and calm.

Note: It is also very useful to do this exercise in conjunction with deep breathing and meditational exercises, which I will describe later on.

3. **Stop the thought in its tracks with a verbal block**

If a thought comes to mind that you recognise as a negative one, immediately say out loud the exact opposite of what the thought is. For example, if you are working towards a deadline and the thought "I'll never make it on time" enters your mind, immediately say out loud (or if in public, whisper to yourself!): "I will make this deadline with plenty of time to spare!" Another technique similar to this is to take the thought to its logical conclusion by asking it: "So what if....?" "So what if I don't meet my deadline, what happens next? And then what after that?" Keep going until you realize that you don't need to stress yourself out with the thought. Whatever happens, you will handle it.

I am sure you will find the above brief exercises useful in your quest. We will go into greater detail on how to analyze and change your thoughts a little later, but for now let's talk about your moods.

Moods: What are they?

A mood is when your mind is focusing and linking all your thoughts that were created and are maintained in a particular frame of mind. Your mind is locking itself into a particular emotion and any thoughts that it associates with that emotion. Neuropsychologists haven't figured out yet exactly how thoughts are linked to each other, but the fact is that thoughts that are created in a particular mood-state will tend to be linked to one another and if you think one of them, it will more than likely lead you to think the others. The negative mood state can be very powerful and if left unchecked can lead one into deep negative states and even depression.

The Negative Mood-State

A negative mood can be one of the most powerful mind-altering states. When I say "mind altering" what I actually mean is thought-altering or thought-pattern altering if you will. The ability of a negative mood-state to induce the recollection and creation of negative thoughts can be both astounding and very unnerving to the person caught in its grip. One negative thought, if left unchecked, can lead to a veritable outpouring of other negative thoughts and, once in this "mood," it becomes quite difficult to extricate oneself into another, more positive mood-state.

Today, some theorists believe that there is something called "mood-state-dependent recall" which means that thoughts that are "recorded" or stored in memory in a particular mood-state will tend to be recalled if that mood-state is active or induced. This would seem to have some validity to it from a purely experiential standpoint. I am sure that you have experienced being in a negative mood-state and have wondered why you suddenly start to think about only the negatives of everything. It can be quite debilitating to be in this kind of state and to start to see everything in a bad light; often thinking negatively about people, places, or situations that you would normally not think negatively about. Theorists believe that certain thoughts are linked by the mood-state in which they were created and thus will tend to be recalled together and reinforce each other while one remains in that particular mood-state. Of course the question is then: How do I get rid of this mood-state and move into a more positive one or even just into a neutral state?

One of the most helpful techniques that I recommend and have used personally when in such a state is to let go and try to create a state of mind that neither accepts nor rejects any thoughts that come to mind. Effectively, what one should try to do is clear the mind or just push "pause" for a while and not worry too much about what thoughts are currently flowing. One of the hardest things to do is to recognise the state and realize that the way you are thinking now, at the moment, is not rational and does not reflect on who you are deep down nor indicate anything about your life and how things are really going right now. There is quite a large amount of guilt and possibly despair that comes with the kind of thoughts that ensue from a deep negative state. These thoughts are not, however, rational and are not the thoughts that one would have in a neutral or positive state. Thus, to blame oneself and degrade oneself for such thoughts is not healthy and will only lead to a lowering of self-esteem. Just accept the thoughts and do not react to them, they will only have meaning and power over you if you allow them to. *It really is your choice to focus on them or let them go.*

When in a negative mood state what you should try to say to yourself is: "I will allow my thoughts to flow through my mind without judging them. I realize that in this state that I am currently in, my thoughts are predominantly negative, out of proportion and probably do not reflect the way I really think or feel about the situation, object, person etc. I will thus decide to refuse these thoughts' power over me and I will ride out this negative state until it has passed and until I am thinking more clearly again".

The worst thing that you can do when in a negative mood-state is to try to make a decision about something important or to talk about issues that are of importance to you. Rather, try to avoid thinking about important issues while in this state. Another thing you should not do is to blame yourself for being in a negative state and to worry about how you will get out of it.

As some psychologists have said, you only make the matter worse by becoming disturbed about your disturbance. The negative state will lift if you let it, so let it. If you try and keep your mind still by letting it run its course, eventually the negative state does recede and you will feel a wonderful feeling of relief as you return to a more neutral frame of mind and with a little effort, a positive and more powerful state of mind!

Tips in dealing with a negative mood

1. Talking it out

One of the most powerful ways to dispel a deep negative mood state that is ingraining itself in your psyche is to talk it out. Find someone you trust, someone you can talk to who you know will listen with empathy and tell him or her what is on your mind and what is bothering you. There is immense power to drain a negative thought pattern in this way, but it must be someone who you know will listen with empathy. If no such person exists, seek a counselling service or a professional therapist who will offer the necessary care and empathy. In Australia today, people have access to a minimum of 12 sessions with a psychologist through the Medicare system and this has allowed a significant number of people to access mental health services who would have previously just continued to suffer on their own without the necessary support.

Keeping your thoughts to yourself and thinking that you show weakness by telling someone about them is dangerous. They will build themselves up and swirl around inside your mind unless they are given release. "Throwing out" your thoughts to someone in this manner is very effective for a number of reasons:

1. In talking to another person and trying to explain to them what you are thinking and feeling, you need to order your thoughts and to make sense of them so that the other person will understand what it is that is bothering you.
2. What this effectively does is force you to catch the most important thoughts that are bothering you and to bring them out into the light of day for objective scrutiny by yourself and your counsellor or friend.

What you may find, after having brought all these thoughts out into the open, is that they are not as bad or as worrisome as you thought they were. The person to whom you have told all this is not caught up in the emotional turmoil of your life and can thus give you a much more objective view of what is happening. Once you hear your own thoughts given back to you in a more objective format, you may see that there really isn't that much to them and that they are not as "bad" or "awful" as you believed them to be. I put bad and awful in quotation marks because these are just labels that we give to our thoughts that do not necessarily reflect their actual content or meaning. What I may label as "bad," you may label as "challenging" or "exciting." It really depends on your perspective.

2. Writing it out

There is another helpful and often-neglected method of relieving a negative mood state and that is getting it down on paper or on a computer. This works on the same principle as talking it out because it forces you to get your thoughts into order and to explain them in a way that makes sense and follows a logical sequence.

There are various ways one can do this:

- You could just sit down, take out a piece of paper and a pen (or log into your computer and open up a Word document), and begin writing down what it is that is troubling you. Here, you just let your mind and hand flow freely and write down whatever it is that is bothering you. You should try to get it down in detail and to not stop until you feel that you have written down each and every thing that is bothering you and is causing you to feel such a negative mood-state. This method also forces you to find out exactly what it is that is bothering you. Sometimes you may have this horrible feeling that something is wrong and can't put a finger on it, but when you actually sit down and think about it, writing your thoughts down on paper or on your computer screen, you find out what it is that is bothering you so much and you can deal with it in a constructive manner.

- Another version of writing it down that can be very effective is to use the "higher self" method. Instead of writing down what is bothering you, you assume that either a close friend, relative, or your own higher self is writing to you. This person or wiser self already knows what is bothering you. (This method is obviously most effective if you have actually written down what is bothering you as in the previous section.) They write you a reply that looks at your worries from an objective and rational viewpoint and they comfort you with words of wisdom about life. You may actually be quite surprised to see the words that you are writing to yourself. Suddenly, you are forcing your mind to think of solutions or ways of making your load lighter because you want to comfort this poor soul whom you care about. Even if you don't care about yourself at the moment, pretend that you do! Write down a response to each thing that is bothering you. You will be amazed at the responses you get from yourself. It's worth a try isn't it? It's just a piece of paper, a pen, and a little bit of your time.

3. Acting it Out

In trying to deal with any kind of problem in life, it would seem that one of the most important things to do is to learn how to act. This may sound like a simple thing to do and yet what one often finds is that in the face of a difficult or even debilitating problem, we tend to avoid doing the very thing that will ensure the resolution of our problem. That thing is to *act,* to *take a positive or constructive step* towards the resolution of our problem no matter how insurmountable it may seem. There is nothing more debilitating than the feeling one gets after spending a day doing absolutely nothing and knowing that one's problems still loom over one's head. Each bit of time that one effectively "hands over" by allowing it to pass by without action is given over to the problem instead of the solution.

Taking this concept of action to its simplest form (the movement of the body), I can vouch for the value of action, almost *any* action, in being able to help one move past one's problems and to lift oneself out of just about any negative mood-state. People who find themselves blocked in their life by what is commonly known as depression often find themselves in a state of complete inertia and inability to take even the simplest action, such as getting out of bed to face the day.

Whether the cause of such debilitation is a chemical imbalance or a dysfunctional way of thinking about the world and themselves, the result of action cannot be denied. The very act of getting out of bed when one feels like there is nothing to get up for puts a point on the positive side of the scale and begins to build self-esteem.

The act of getting dressed, making breakfast and then doing an activity (any constructive activity!), adds more points to the positive side. Sitting and brooding about one's life and trying to think one's way out of a deep negative state or depression will very rarely produce positive results. When the problem you are in has been caused because of your thinking, sometimes you cannot use that same mode to get yourself back out again. You may need a jump-start first, just as a dead car battery needs that jolt of energy from another battery to get started and begin charging itself again.

Getting oneself to go out and do something productive, no matter what that thing may be, will lead one to feel energized and this in turn will lead to new ideas, new possibilities and a renewed sense of well being. It is a case of action leading to thought instead of the usual thought leading to action. If one has been blocked by one avenue (in the case of depression or negative states, that avenue is our own thoughts), then one needs to look for another avenue that may lead us to the destination that we seek by helping us to get around the blockage. The avenue that is open is the one of action.

Combining the avenue of action with the other techniques above and the detailed techniques you will learn a little later on will have an immense effect on your thoughts and subsequently your beliefs. With a change in your core beliefs and the way you see the world and what is possible for you in it, you will notice the much-desired change in your outer reality. The world changes towards you if you take the steps to change towards it. As Merlin in Deepak Chopra's book *The Way of the Wizard* says:

"You cannot bring the same stale self to the world and expect the world to be new for you!"

Think about it and change your mind.

CHAPTER 3 — THE CONSCIOUS
WAY TO CHANGE YOUR MIND

Some people don't like the idea of working with the subconscious mind directly. When I have offered to help people work with their innermost beliefs and thoughts through hypnosis, some of them either don't believe that it works or they feel that they cannot let go of their defences enough to let someone get that close to their real selves. They will often say things like: "You can't hypnotise me, no one has ever been able to hypnotise me!" And the funny thing is that they are right. I won't be able to hypnotise them because as soon as they have set up their subconscious mind to believe that they cannot be hypnotised, no one will ever be able to get them into hypnosis. Their subconscious mind will actually prevent them from letting it happen because it has been told that it cannot be done or that it needs to protect them from it. Believing that you can benefit from hypnosis and being open to it is also just a belief that can be created that the subconscious mind will take at face value.

I do not work very often using hypnosis. If one uses the techniques that I will describe in this chapter in conjunction with hypnosis, the results are going to be very quick and effective. However, having said that, some people like to work at a slower pace that they feel more comfortable with, and that's fine too. I will explain to these people that the harder they work at it, using these tools consciously every day, the quicker they will be able to create lasting and effective change in their lives.

As explained in the previous chapter, the first step in learning to change your mind is to begin to have awareness. This awareness is an internal awareness of your "state of mind" on a continuous basis and that would involve careful attention to what you are thinking. Your thoughts are the keys to your beliefs and to the reasons your life is the way it is at the present moment. Everything starts with your thoughts. The first major breakthrough and success you will have as you begin this journey is to become *aware.*

Many people go through life unaware of how their thinking controls so much in their lives. They don't think about thinking! They are on automatic pilot and work from a very externally focused point of view. They view the events in their lives as having direct impact on them and their emotions without considering there may be a part which thinking plays in how they feel and how they respond to everything in their lives. And of course, they would never stop, take a step back from their own thinking, and review the content of their minds. They don't question the validity of their interpretation of events. If something happens to them that is "bad," they must naturally just feel bad and act accordingly. But there is another way, a much better way that provides more control over your thoughts, emotions, and behaviours in life. And the outcome of this is the achievement of what you want, the attainment of great peace of mind, and subsequently lower levels of anxiety, stress, and depression. This is what I try to achieve with every client I see for counselling. With the application of the tools and techniques you are about to learn in this chapter and the rest of this book, you too can attain these same results.

Most people believe that the sequence or chain of events that occurs with regards to themselves and their environment goes something like this:

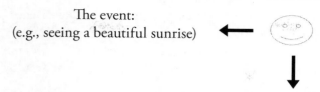

The event:
(e.g., seeing a beautiful sunrise)

The Outcome: I feel great! That *makes* me feel good!

The actual sequence of events (shown below) would be more fully stated in the following way:

The Outcome: I feel great! That *makes* me feel good!

When you see the "activating" event (the sunrise in this case), it wouldn't mean anything to you unless you had some thought about it. If you were distracted by something else at the time and you were thinking about something horrible that had happened, you might not even notice the sunrise, much less feel really good about seeing it. This goes to show that it is not the actual event outside yourself that "causes" you to have an emotional reaction of feeling good. It is you, through your seeing that sunrise, making sense out of it in your mind and attaching value and meaning to it that sets up the emotion or feelings that create that wonderful feeling inside when you see a beautiful sunset.

Most of the time the sequence of events, thoughts, beliefs, and emotional reactions occur so quickly that we aren't even aware that it's happening. Through years of "thinking without thinking," we have pretty much let life happen to us and let ourselves experience any emotion or feeling that happens to come up from there. What you are going to learn now is that you have so much more power to control your thoughts, beliefs, and emotional states than you would ever have believed possible.

For now, it is a great step just to realize that most of your thinking up to now has been automatic. It happens without much of your own conscious awareness and without you working on choosing the thoughts that you want to have. As explained earlier, you can start to write down your thoughts and keep a thought journal so that you can start to work with your thoughts. If something happens to you, let's say you get stuck in a traffic jam, and you immediately feel frustrated and irritated, stop for a second and think over the thoughts you have had from before the traffic jam until you got into it. You were feeling pretty good and enjoying your day, thinking about the nice movie you saw last night and then you noticed the traffic jam up ahead. What were your exact thoughts as soon as you saw the jam? Make a mental note of those thoughts and write them down as soon as you can so you can examine them later using the techniques to follow.

They might go something like this:

"I can't believe this! Now I am going to be late for work and get into trouble with the boss. Why does this always happen to me? What a horrible way to start the day!"

Right! Now you have caught your first thought pattern. It's like a game of fishing with the event acting as your bait to bring out your habitual thoughts and beliefs! You could even turn it into a game if you want as this may help you not take the whole process too seriously and it will help you see the funny side and avoid being pulled down by your emotions too much. Once you have compiled a rough set of thoughts that have caused you trouble throughout the previous days or maybe weeks, you can then sit down and begin to work with them with the techniques below. Before we go into them however, I would like to give you some background on the following methods to change your mind.

As described earlier in the book, the field of cognitive psychology and later rational-emotive behavior therapy began in the 1950s and quickly spread throughout the psychology profession as it gained more and more popularity.

I believe that part of the reason it spread so quickly and established itself as a highly influential movement within the psychotherapy communities was that it was just so effective. The time frames for recovery of clients were shorter and major improvements in mood disorders were seen when the cognitive-behavioural approach was used.

In the introduction to his book *Feeling Good: A New Mood Therapy*[2], Dr. David Burns, a prominent psychiatrist, describes how the techniques used by cognitive psychologists have been tested experimentally with groups of depressed patients. The patients were divided into groups. Some were given anti-depressants only, some were given anti-depressants and cognitive-behavioural treatment and others were only given cognitive-behavioural treatment. The amazing results of this study showed that the patients who only had cognitive-behavioural therapy improved more dramatically and stayed better (as detailed in follow-up studies years later) than both of the other groups!

Dr. Burns showed just how effective the conscious method of dealing with your thoughts, moods, beliefs, and behaviors can be. I have used the techniques and tools firstly in my own life and secondly to help others when they have approached me for counselling. I know how effective they are and that is why I would like to share them with you — along with the other ideas, techniques and methods that will be outlined in the rest of the book — because I have seen how they can transform a person's life from abnormally low self-esteem to a healthy, reasonable self-esteem. I have seen it break down and cure phobias (from being terrified of flying in a plane to being petrified of mice and rats). I have seen it lift people out of depression and I have seen it help people who suffer from anxiety start to lead normal, peaceful, and calmer lives.

---

2 Burns, D.1991. Feeling Good: A New Mood Therapy. New York: Harper Collins

As I have said, the research behind the methods was developed working with people who suffered from depression, but these tools and techniques can be (and have been) used to help people from all walks of life with any manner of problems facing them. We all need to work on our thoughts and we all get ourselves into a little trouble here and there when we let our thoughts rule our lives and control all our emotions. From the employee who thinks that no one likes him or her and that people are always laughing behind his or her back, to the lady who wants to be the perfect mother and keeps losing the battle of being perfect — ridiculing herself and blaming herself for not being able to do it all. We all have our demons and thoughts that haunt us every now and then that make our lives more difficult and sometimes seemingly too difficult to handle. But there is always a way to see it from a different angle and fundamentally change your perception about what is going on and what things mean to you. When you learn to master your thoughts, you will master your emotions and your destiny.

Dr. Albert Ellis and later Dr. Aaron T. Beck explained that our thought patterns and beliefs worked so quickly in any given situation that the thoughts that cross our minds on a day-to-day basis are practically automatic in nature. We don't realize what we are thinking until we have an emotional reaction to it. The negative automatic thoughts or, rearranged, ANTS (automatic negative thoughts), that we have can run across our minds so fast — literally like incredibly fast little ANTS — that we don't take any notice of them. After many years of working with the types of thoughts and grouping of thoughts that people have (especially the kinds of thoughts that depressed people have), Dr. Beck developed categories that most of them seemed to fall into. These categories are also known as *cognitive distortions*. These categories are extremely useful when you want to see whether a thought you have had is realistic and rational or whether it is an irrational and negative thought that needs to be reviewed and changed.

Just before we get into the actual categories I want to provide you with a quick little acid test that you can use when you need to check whether your thoughts are helping you or harming you. First catch the thought you are having and then ask yourself these three questions:

1. Do I know if this thought is 100 percent true and accurate?
2. Is this thought useful?
3. Does this thought help me achieve any of my immediate goals?

If you answer no to any of these questions, you probably need to look at discarding the thought and thinking of some alternatives.

OK, so here are the categories of thoughts you need to study and get to know very well.

The 10 major categories of distorted thoughts

1. Fortune Telling and Mind Reading

Let's take **Mind Reading** first. We all do this to a greater or lesser extent every day. I know that I often have to remind myself when I am using this mental distortion and to force myself to hold off on judging a situation or a person until real, hard facts and evidence present themselves to justify any thoughts I may have. When you are using this mental distortion or when it is happening in your mind, you often mistakenly think that you can tell what other people are thinking about you. You might meet someone for the first time and think that that person probably has a certain opinion of you, that they have judged you in a certain way. For example, that person is really good looking and you imagine that they think you are beneath them and not worth talking to. In response, you decide that you won't approach them or be open to them as a human being and a possible friend or romantic interest. That is the concept of mind reading. If you catch yourself thinking that you just "know" what that person is thinking about you, think again. Unless you have some psychic abilities that the rest of us don't have and you can hear what people are thinking, then you need to learn to hold off on imagining what they think. You need to take a step back, remind yourself to be objective and not to judge. Rather be open to that person and to anything that may come of your encounter with that person. We can often miss out on some really great relationships, business associates, and lovers if we don't learn to silence the mind- reading maniac we all seem to have in our heads. We love to just imagine what the other person is thinking or feeling and then we go right ahead and respond to that person as if they had really said or felt what we think they did! I used to think that those soap operas were overly dramatic when they showed someone imagining what their lover was thinking or doing and then getting all upset over their imaginings, but guess what — it's true to life! We all do this.

Next, let's discuss the cognitive distortion of **Fortune Telling**. This one is pretty straightforward. It means that we try to predict what will happen in the future. Any time you or I try to imagine what will happen and predict the course of life, we may be setting ourselves up for a disappointment. Alternatively, we may be pleasantly surprised by an outcome we could never have predicted. Life does work like that; we plan, we strategize and try and think about all the possible outcomes of a particular course of action but we can never really be sure which way it's going to go. People who use this distortion will commonly say things to themselves such as: "I'll never make the team," "It's not worth trying because I know I am going to be rejected anyway," "What's the point of going to this party? I know I'm not going to meet anyone and I'll probably just have a lousy time." It's a simple one to recognise as being faulty or irrational thinking, but so few people actually look at these thoughts and say to themselves that the thoughts are irrational. They will often believe the thought and then act on their belief in that thought being their objective reality. The truth is that we just never can tell what will happen, who we will meet, how good a time we are going to have, how successful our efforts will be, unless we go out there and try or unless we actually get there and see for ourselves whether what we thought would happen actually did happen. Again, be careful of this because if you continue to believe hard enough that something will happen, positive or negative, it might just happen. Affirm a positive outcome and go and see for yourself — without any preconceived ideas — that's what it's all about.

You can see from the two explanations above of Mind Reading and Fortune-Telling why they fall into the same category. It's because in each instance you are trying to predict or imagine what someone is thinking or that something will happen, without any objective facts to support your prediction or imagination.

2. Negative Mental Filter

This distortion of the **Negative Mental Filter** is like a net that we have thrown across the river of our lives. While everything goes through the net, such as the evidence of good things in our lives and the everyday positives and things we have to be happy about — we have set our nets to catch only the "bad" or negative things that happen to us. Whenever we look at our life or a particular situation in it, we focus on everything that is wrong with it. We ignore the good and the positive and let it slip through our nets (our filter) without a trace. So much of life is really all about what you focus on and what you give meaning to. It's all about your own perspective and how you rate events and situations. When we use a Negative Mental Filter, we actively see only the negative. We often don't even try to see the good or positive things in our lives. All you need to do when you find yourself using this cognitive distortion is learn to take the filter off (like taking a pair of dirty glasses off) and view your life more objectively — the good and the "bad". Give your focus and filter a good cleaning out so that you are able to see both sides of the coin and learn to be more objective and rational about your life. To go one better, I would say that you should create a pair of glasses (or a mental filter) that is skewed to filter more positive into your life. You should be actively seeking out and focusing more on the positives than the negatives. It takes just the same amount of effort as the Negative Mental Filter and it is a lot more beneficial to you. I am not saying that you need to become delusional and have visions of grandeur, but I am saying that life is full of positives, of things to be happy about and grateful for, and it just makes much more sense to focus on those than to focus on all the perceived negatives in your life. That's really changing your mind!

3. All-or-Nothing Thinking

When you are using this cognitive distortion you see the world only in terms of right or wrong, black or white, yes and no, winners and losers. **All-or-Nothing Thinking** does not allow for the in-between, the gray areas in life. It also leaves no room for improvement and is very critical of any errors or anything that is not "perfect." There are people who think that they won't try doing something unless they can be really good at it, otherwise what's the point, right? By scrutinizing that kind of thinking we can see that it's the kind of thinking used by perfectionists and perfectionists tend to be very hard on themselves and others as well and usually become very tense and stressed out. People who use this type of distorted thinking most probably had quite harsh parents who weren't happy unless they were achieving the highest marks or the best results. Their outer critics (their parents) became inner critics in the form of a script in their heads or a little voice that says to them that they aren't good enough unless they are the best. It is a very harsh way of thinking and it can kill any kind of motivation before it begins. The fear of not doing or being the best or at least being very good is far larger than the idea of just enjoying what you are doing — no matter how much you suck at it! I like the idea that there is *no such thing as failure and* *that there are only results* (thanks Tony Robbins!). That's a brilliant belief to cultivate, an excellent way to change your mind, because when you have this belief going for you, you cannot lose. You can always be somewhere on the ladder of achievement and results and you can always take a step higher. There are very few cut and dried issues in the world. Many things are open for debate — why should your so-called "failures" be any different. You have not failed; you have only achieved a certain set of results. They may not be what you wanted, but you can always try again tomorrow, or the next day, and keep improving and changing until you achieve what you want. Don't black or white your life or anything in it, color it in all the wonderful colors of the rainbow. Life is very rich and varied, so there is no need to see things in only black or white.

4. Catastrophisng (Magnifying and Minimizing)

When we use this cognitive distortion, we are in effect blowing things out of proportion or conversely making things seem smaller than they really are. The funny thing is that we use magnification, or **Catastrophisng,** for all the bad things in our lives and we use minimization for all the good. Dr. David Burns calls this the "binocular trick" because it's like looking through the wrong side of a binoculars when we look at ourselves and our achievements — in which case they seem rather small and insignificant, and we look at our problems and our mistakes or faults with the magnifying side of the binoculars — in which case we blow them way out of proportion to their real size. Anyone would begin to feel absolutely miserable if they did this on a continuous basis. It's like using anything you can to make yourself feel worthless and useless while minimizing or even totally ignoring your good or even excellent qualities! What a ridiculous thing to do to yourself and yet so many people do it, every day. I do it, my patients do it, we all do it to some extent and the trick is to learn when we are doing it and push ourselves to stop it.

5. Emotional Reasoning

This distortion is quite a strong one, as it not only involves what you are thinking but also is integrally linked to your emotions. **Emotional Reasoning** is when you take the saying: "I think, therefore I am" and change it to: "I feel, therefore it is so." You decide that because you feel a certain way at the moment, your circumstances, your life must be actually that bad. You may be feeling low for whatever reason and because you are physically and emotionally low, you tend to assume that something must be really wrong with your life. The problem with emotional reasoning is that it feeds back into your thoughts and beliefs and can lead into a negative spiral if you aren't careful about catching yourself when you are doing it. Don't make the mistake of thinking that because you feel a certain way, your life is going down the tubes and all is lost! When you have worked with the thoughts and taken some physical action, as we will discuss in another chapter, you will find that your feelings will lift and you will start to think much more positively and rationally about your life. There may even be times when you cannot believe how negatively you were thinking and feeling about everything in your life, even something as simple as burning the toast in the morning! One of the biggest bits of advice to you when you are in the middle of an emotional reasoning distortion and negativity cycle is to never allow yourself to think about anything important in your life. Don't try to make any decisions about your life, either. When you are on this emotional roller coaster, it's best to sit it out and wait until you are able to think more clearly before making any life changing decisions. Just accept that it is a little emotional storm and it will pass if you don't get too caught up in it. By using some of the techniques described in this book, you should be able to pull yourself out of it quite quickly.

6. Labeling

When you **Label** something or someone, you are in effect limiting that object or person to the label you have given. Your label may not be accurate, but once labelled; you may feel compelled to stick to it, no matter how much evidence there may be to the contrary. This is especially irrational when it comes to people, and especially ourselves, because we are so dynamic and changing that to label ourselves as stupid, clumsy, lazy and other such terms does not reflect the whole truth. I cannot say that because I didn't pick up my clothes this morning that this means I am a sloth and a lazy, good-for-nothing idiot, can I? Some people might say that I could and that it would be justified. The problem is that I am using one action (or inaction in this case) to label myself — my whole personality and everything that goes with it — as lazy and good-for-nothing. I am sure that if I went back in my mind, I could find plenty of evidence for just the opposite of being a lazy, good-for-nothing idiot. I am sure I could find times when I diligently went about cleaning up after myself and when I even helped to clean the whole house. This would be evidence that would be in contradiction to the label I gave myself and so this is why the label and the act of labeling is a cognitive distortion. In cognitive psychology there is another term for this type of activity that is known as stereotyping. When you stereotype yourself or someone else, you in effect take a little bit of information about that person or yourself and use it to class them or categorize them as a particular type. You may do this in your mind to help simplify information and to help you understand your world faster, but it is not necessarily the best way to sort information in your brain and come to any realistic conclusions. This is because your conclusions would be based on very little factual information and would hardly stand up to the scrutiny of a scientific approach to fact finding! Another point to remember is that when someone else has done something that you don't like, let's say they stood on your toe in the line in the bank, for example: if you were to swear at them in your head and label them a clumsy idiot, that would be a cognitive distortion. It would be much more accurate to say that their behavior or the action that they took in that moment was a bit clumsy but that does not say anything about them as a person. You should much rather label the behavior than the person. This would especially apply to the way a parent talks to a child. If you label your child stupid when he does something you don't think is right and you actually say to him: "How can you be so stupid!" you are labeling your child instead of labeling the behavior. I am sure I don't have to tell you how damaging such remarks would be to a child or teenager. If you need to say something, it would be much more rational to say to your child: "What you just *did* was not thoughtful and I know you are usually a more thoughtful person. What you just *did* was not right, but I am sure you will *do* it right next time." I know that might sound long-winded, but I am sure you get the general idea. Don't apply meaningless labels to yourself or others, it doesn't help them or you, in fact, it will probably just get your own or other people's emotions out of whack for nothing!

7. **Personalisation**

When you **Personalize** a situation or incident, what you are in effect doing is blaming yourself for something that was never in your direct control, physically or mentally. This would include your perceived control over what others do. People will often attribute negative events to themselves and positive events to outside influences such as luck or coincidence. This is also known as false attribution. When you blame yourself for negative events in your life, which you had no direct control over, you are personalizing them and causing yourself a great deal of unnecessary guilt. As Dr. Burns explains in his book: you may have some influence over people (especially if you are their teacher, parent or friend) but you cannot control their thoughts and their actions. What they do is their own full responsibility and should not leave you feeling responsible or guilt-ridden. Most of the time all you can do is offer your advice and support. People tend to do what they want to do anyway, so blaming yourself is not going to help the situation and is most probably not an accurate reflection of the situation. This applies equally to situations or events that happen in your life that you have no real control over. This often leads into the thinking of: "If only I had…" and can lead to terrible guilt and remorse that is mostly unfounded.

8. **Should Statements**

We all do this. We all like to motivate ourselves by saying: "I really should do this" or "I really have to get going with that. **Should Statements** also involve the use of the following words:

- Must
- Better (as in "I better get it done")
- Ought to

These are not very motivating words and they often only create pressure and tension in our minds. By telling yourself you "better do this" or you "have to do that" you place yourself under emotional strain and unless you do what you're told (even if it's telling yourself!) it feels like there will be dire consequences. Who wants to live with that kind or tirade going on in their heads? We had parents and teachers who did this for us when we were young, why on earth would we want to carry it on in our own heads when we become adults? Some people do. They think that that is how they can get the best out of themselves and motivate themselves to get going. Let's take a look at some other words that we could use that may be more motivating, less harsh and easier on the stomach lining!

- I *want* to…
- I would *like* to…
- I *enjoy*…
- I *am going* to…

Much better! I *would rather* use those words than any of the others above them. One writer called the cognitive distortion of Should Statements, "should'ing on yourself"!

What we need to realize in coming to grips with this distortion, is that there are very few things we really *have to* do. We always have options, even if those options may not get us the best or most friendly results. We may feel that we have to go and get some milk and bread for the house, but by telling ourselves "I have to go and get milk and bread," it really makes it sound like a chore doesn't it? We don't really have to do it, do we? We could, if we so chose, not go and get the milk and bread. No one is holding a gun to our heads to go and get it. Sometimes we put ourselves in an imaginary prison cell where our lives are restricted and we don't have any options. That is a very stressful and unintelligent way to live, especially when we do it to ourselves!

Overall, I have found that whenever I catch myself "shoulding" on myself and trying to get myself to take action that way, it is always easier to use the softer words, the more motivating words. Try it for yourself, it works wonders for the digestion!

9. Overgeneralisation

We're nearly there now! When using **Overgeneralisation**, we are taking one example of something that has happened to us either now or in the past, and are using that example as evidence of how it is always going to be in the future. In a way this is a similar distortion to Mind Reading and Fortune Telling in terms of us trying to predict what will happen. We stop ourselves from trying again because we think that because it happened once, twice, or even three times, it is bound to happen again and that we now have evidence enough to prove that we are useless (Labeling!) or that we cannot achieve something we have set our hearts on achieving (Fortune Telling!). As you can see, the cognitive distortions can often be intermingled and linked to each other and one line of thinking may have more than one cognitive distortion in it. The more distortions you can find in your line of thinking, the more obvious it should be to you that you are thinking in irrational ways and that you need to identify and change your thoughts and beliefs

10. Disqualifying the Positive

This final cognitive distortion, **Disqualifying the Positive**, is very similar to the one on the negative mental filter. The difference is that, whereas with the negative mental filter you only focus on the negative and you tend to ignore the positive, with this distortion you are made aware of the positive or you can see the positive for yourself, but you make the decision that the positive happened by chance, luck, coincidence or anything else you fancy. You resolutely refuse to see that the evidence you have of the positive is directly disputing your negative or faulty belief. You dismiss the positive and decide that the real objective truth is found in the negative (or what you may call the "realistic") evidence you have about your world! Can you believe we do this to ourselves? You bet we do.

How it works in practice

When you find a thought or pattern of thoughts that have been distressing you, nine out of ten times you will find that they fall into one of these categories. If the thought doesn't fall into any of these categories, it may be rational, in which case you will then need to find a better way to deal with the situation or emotion. This is when the rest of the techniques in this book will be helpful because we cannot deny that there may be situations and events that are real and cannot be classified as merely irrational thinking. You may then need to find other ways to change your mind and your emotions (assuming they need changing at all at that particular time). As I have said, this is why I have decided to include a variety of methods to help you change your mind and your life because one should never only rely on one approach, especially if there is a definite benefit to using another technique. I believe in using whatever works for you and whatever you find the most effective in helping you improve your life and changing anything you want to change. As they say, "If the shoe fits, wear it!"

A Case Study — Why do bad things always happen to me?!
Lets go back to the lady I described earlier who had the belief entrenched in her mind that she was the cause of all the bad things that happened to her and anyone she loved. When we were early into her counselling, we worked with an incident that had happened to her the week before. Her mobile phone had been stolen in a shopping mall and when she realised it had been stolen, she got so upset she couldn't stop crying for hours. Now, most people would find an event like this very upsetting to say the least. However, most people would be able to get past the event after a day or two and they would also not come out with the thoughts that this young lady did when I asked her to remember exactly what she thought just after the incident occurred. They went something like this:

"I can't believe this has happened, it's all my fault"

"It's just my luck, this always happens to me. Nobody else has such bad luck"

"I brought this on myself because I am a bad person"

"God hates me and he is punishing me."

Wow, now those are not just ANTS she is dealing with, those thoughts are silent killers and have the potential to be very damaging and even lethal because they indicate an underlying belief system that is filled with distortions, half-truths, and outright lies about any objective reality of the situation. Can you imagine the emotions that accompanied this little tyranny of destructive thoughts and beliefs? She was an emotional wreck and every time something like this happened, she used it to verify that her beliefs were true because negative events like this truly seemed to be attracted to her. As I explained earlier, be very careful what you put into your subconscious mind because it will create your reality and it will even act as a self-fulfilling prophesy as it did for this young lady.

Now, let's see how we dealt with those thoughts using the categories above as a guideline.

Starting with the first thought:

"I can't believe this has happened, it's all my fault."

This thought falls into the category of **Personalisation** for something that was completely out of her own physical and mental control. It is very self-defeating to blame herself for something she could not have avoided. If she had been careless and had been walking around with her handbag wide open with her mobile phone in plain view, then there is the possibility that there was some element of her own fault involved. But, these thieves, being professionals, could have taken the phone off anyone, even a security-conscious person, so there was really no basis for her thoughts that the theft of her phone was her own fault. It would have been much more helpful to her psychologically if she had gotten mad at them for stealing her phone than to get upset and blame herself for what happened. So we caught that thought, recognised it as a thought that belonged to the cognitive distortion of Personalisation, and then we disputed the thought with a more rational belief about what happened.

There is a specific tool that you can use for working with your thoughts — I call it the thought worksheet. I have included a copy for you in the appendix.

During counselling with this young lady, we used the thought worksheet and this is how it came out for her:

Trigger	ANT	Emotion	Behavioural Reaction	Label	PAT	% Belief in PAT
Mobile phone stolen	"I can't believe this has happened, it's all my fault"	Despondent Angry Frustrated Humiliated Upset	Crying Shaking Lashed out at friends Screamed at the cat	**Personalisation:** The thought that was identified fell into this category of cognitive distortions	I am usually very careful, besides, it could've happened to anyone. It's not my fault that thieves stole from me!	60%

Now, you may notice that she only gave it a 60 percent belief in terms of her truly believing the PAT as opposed to the ANT. This is, however, a major step forward and many people may have even put a 10 percent or 20 percent belief in the PAT. Remember what I said earlier: you don't have to believe the new thoughts or beliefs right away. Just the act of writing down your thoughts and working with them in this way helps you to shed light on what is going on in your mind and helps you start to feel better pretty quickly. The best thing about writing it out in this fashion is that whenever you have the thoughts again and you identify them as the same thoughts and beliefs, you don't have to do the work all over again, you can just pull out your journal and read through what you wrote the last time. Or, if you prefer, you could rewrite what you wrote and just give a new percentage belief in the PAT. What you will find as you keep at it is that those percentages will start to increase and you will start believing in the PATs as opposed to the ANTs. The stronger your negative thoughts and beliefs and the more entrenched they are, the more you might have to keep repeating the alternative thoughts. I would like to suggest that you not only write it out, but that once you have that positive, more rational thought written down, you say it out loud and with some conviction. Hearing the positive statements being spoken by your own voice can be very powerful and will engage you with the thought even more.

Take a look at the second thought she had:

"It's just my luck, this always happens to me. Nobody else has such bad luck."

You can see from this thought that there are some underlying beliefs going on here. "This always happens to me" would indicate that she believes there is something about herself that attracts negative events (and possibly people) into her life. What label would you give this thought? If someone is saying that something *always* happens to him or her and that it *never* happens to anyone else, they are using the cognitive distortion of... Overgeneralisation! Why? Because Overgeneralisation is when you take a single event and generalize it to your whole life.

Let's see how it looks on paper:

Trigger	ANT	Emotion	Behavioural Reaction	Label	PAT	% Belief in PAT
Mobile phone stolen	"It's just my luck, this always happens to me. Nobody else has such bad luck"	Despondent Angry Frustrated Humiliated Upset	Crying Shaking Lashed out at friends Screamed at the cat	**Overgeneralisation:** The thought that was identified fell into this category of cognitive distortions	I have never actually had my mobile phone stolen before. It definitely does happen to a lot of other people. Negative things do happen, but I can't say whether it's because I have bad luck!	50%

The third thought was:

"I brought this on myself because I am a bad person."

This one may involve two different cognitive distortions: Personalisation and Labeling. It can be classified as Personalisation because she is again blaming herself for something that was out of her control and it can also

44

be called labeling because she has referred to herself as a bad person from an event that could never really indicate anything about her intrinsic "goodness" or "badness." As Dr. Burns says, we cannot try to define ourselves with labels like these. We are very complex and to try to label ourselves as good, bad, ugly, etc., is not possible because we are so much more than a label. We cannot fit into such a narrow classification of who we are, what we think and how we feel.

Working with this thought, we would have a table like this:

Trigger	ANT	Emotion	Behavioural Reaction	Label	PAT	% Belief in PAT
Mobile phone stolen	"I brought this on myself because I am a bad person."	Despondent Angry at Self Frustrated Humiliated Upset	Crying Shaking Lashed out at friends Screamed at the cat	**Personalisation and Labeling:** The thought that was identified fell into these two categories of cognitive distortions	I am not a bad person. Nothing I did in this situation was my own fault. I cannot say I am bad because I am too complex a person to be labelled so easily and I have many good and kind qualities too.	70%

She could see more clearly (and she even laughed out loud a bit) with this one that it didn't mean she was bad and had no bearing whatsoever on who she was as a human being.

The final thought was:

"God hates me and he is punishing me."

As discussed under the category of Mind Reading, we cannot know what anyone is thinking, and that would definitely include God! If we cannot even know what the people who are closest to us are really thinking, how could we ever propose to know and understand what God is thinking and why things happen in life the way they do. We may, in hindsight, see why something happened to us and what we needed to learn from it and then possibly infer that that was what God wanted us to learn or understand, but we cannot say for any certainty what God has in mind for us. Of course this is assuming that you believe in God or a higher power in the universe.

Let's look at the worksheet:

Trigger	ANT	Emotion	Behavioural Reaction	Label	PAT	% Belief in PAT
Mobile phone stolen	"God hates me and he is punishing me"	Despondent Sad Humiliated Upset Lost Confused Hopeless	Crying Shaking Lashed out at friends Screamed at the cat	**Mind Reading:** The thought that was identified fell into these two categories of cognitive distortions	I really have no way of knowing why this happened to me at this moment. It happened for a reason, which I may understand sometime in the future. I am not a bad person, God doesn't hate me — hate is a human emotion.	70%

Although it can be difficult to go into this type of exercise when religious beliefs are involved, it is still possible to work with rational thinking to help avoid any irrational and negative beliefs a person might have about her life.

The above examples should give you a fairly good idea of the process that you can use to work with your thoughts. As mentioned previously, I have included a worksheet at the back of the book that you can use for your thought work. I would suggest that you get yourself a hardcover book that will become your thought journal, where you can begin to take note of the thoughts that you have when you find yourself feeling down or emotionally on edge. Remember, it all starts with becoming aware of your thinking. Don't get upset with yourself for thinking irrationally or if you slip and you find yourself thinking negative thoughts. The first step is to be able to recognise when you are thinking using a cognitive distortion. Always give yourself a pat on the back for catching a negative thought or mood. This will encourage you to keep at it, even if you aren't an expert yet at dealing with those thoughts using the above system. In time, as you work more and more with writing the thoughts down and disputing them, those particular thoughts and beliefs will begin to change and soon you will no longer need to work with them on paper because you will have cut a new groove in your brain — a new neural pathway — that will automatically dispute the negative thought or belief and assert your new positive and rational beliefs and thoughts. You will be amazed at just how effective this process can be and how quickly it can change how you feel about your life. I encourage you to give it a try and to be patient with yourself and the process. If you need some help with it, I am happy to respond to e-mails.

CHAPTER 4 — DEALING WITH
NEGATIVE EMOTION

We all know how powerful our emotions can be. They sometimes seem to take on a life of their own and leave us feeling out of control. There are times when you won't be able to get yourself out of negative emotions by thinking your way out. I have had to learn this lesson a few times before it finally sunk in that it's true. There is a direct correlation between how bad you feel physically and how negative and depressing your thoughts can be. If, for example, you come down with the flu and you really feel down physically and your levels of energy are very low, it is very likely that you will also feel a corresponding low sense of overall well-being that will influence your thoughts. I have noticed this time and again whenever I come down with the flu or when I am physically tired or irritable. I feel physically down and it clouds my thoughts and my reasoning to such an extent that I might actually start to believe the load of rubbish that is going on inside my head! I'm really learning that this is a one-way street to misery and unhappiness. What goes on inside your mind when you are physically low is a big show about how miserable and horrible your life is and that there is no end in sight!

What we are actually doing in these instances is basing our thoughts about our reality around how we are *currently* feeling without any reference or even the ability to reference the objective reality of our lives. This is called emotional reasoning (i.e., I feel therefore it must be so!) You think that just because you feel bad, things must be really bad. And the more you try and think your way out, the more you think about your life, the more the negative irrational thoughts keep flowing through your head! So, what can we do about it?

There is a cardinal rule when it comes to these types of situations and it's very complicated, so read carefully and get your pen and paper out. The cardinal rule when you feel so low and your life just looks like a bad movie that won't end is…...

STOP THINKING!

Don't spend one more minute trying to think your way out of it. Just stop thinking. Make the decision — and you can even tell yourself verbally — that you have decided for the rest of the day to not think about anything important. How easy is it to do? It's damn hard, let me tell you, but it's well worth the effort and the resulting feeling of letting go and relaxing about your life. There may be a hundred real issues that you may need to deal with, but when you are really physically not at your best, you have to make the mental decision to avoid thinking about anything that is of major importance in your life. I call these days "mind-stop" or "cruise control" days. Slip your mind into neutral and just let the day happen by itself.

If you want to think about something, think about a movie you've seen recently or a funny thing that happened to you the other day. Think about your dog or a beautiful place you've been to. Run back a mental movie of yourself walking through the woods or sitting on the beach watching the waves. Or even better yet, don't think, picture, or visualise anything at all! Do you think you could do that? Like I said, it's not easy, but it can be done. There's no doubt that it can be done. It's a skill that you can learn like any other skill — the ability to just be, to not judge your life or anything in it for a few hours. If you are working on something, just focus on that one thing. If you are taking the dog for a walk, just focus on doing that activity. It's like Zen Buddhism — you know, the concept of "when I am chopping wood, I am chopping wood and when I am carrying water, I am carrying water." I am *not* carrying water and thinking about the hundred and one things I need to do tomorrow or how horrible I feel or how hopeless everything feels at the moment. JUST STOP IT! The opposite of the Nike slogan! Be easy on yourself. When you feel that low physically and emotionally, you need to treat yourself well. You need to take some action that will nourish your soul and make you feel good about yourself. Take a hot bath, go for a long walk, take a ride on your bike, or play with your pet if you have one (that's my favourite). By doing these things for yourself and taking care of yourself as a parent would a child who is sick, you will find that after a while you "wake up" from this world of just being and doing and you feel remarkably better. You feel more calm, more centered and at peace with your life. The reason is, you have given yourself that much-needed mental break from the incessant negativity going on in your mind and your mind calms down and allows itself to be more positive and focus on other things.

Just recently I had a prime example of this when I was having quite a bad day and was really feeling frustrated and down emotionally. There was nothing really major going on in my external world that would lead to me feeling like this, so I knew that I had to take action and that I had been spending too much time in my head and not enough time using my body and being out in the world. So I immediately stopped what I was doing, got into exercise clothes and went for a bike ride. After a thirty-minute bike ride, a few push-ups and sit-ups (which I never do enough of), and a cool shower, I felt completely different. My thoughts were now spinning with ideas and possibilities. My energy levels were up and I was clearly in a much better place emotionally to carry on with the day. It works, I know it and you know it too.

I am not saying that one should avoid emotion and feeling one's emotions. Not at all. There are times when you can, and indeed must, tap into your emotions and feel them fully because to bottle them up and try to avoid feeling any emotion is very dangerous for your mental well-being. Genuine emotion, which is related to a stressful life event, should be felt and dealt with. We all need to go through the process of grieving and healing in order to move on in a healthy manner from any sad or tragic event in our lives.

Even in these times, however, one may get to a point where the body and mind need a break from all the pain and the hurt and this is where the practicing of "just being" can be helpful. Even if it's only for a few hours, it can be very necessary and helpful to decide to stop thinking for a few hours and just be.

On a lighter note, this technique of "thought-stopping" can be utilized anytime, anywhere. Whenever you feel like you just need a break from all the thinking going on inside your head, just make the decision to stop. Start a process of being aware of your thoughts instead of just letting them ride roughshod around in your mind like some crazy motorcycle gang on drugs, and then begin to let them go and let them leave your mind. Imagine that you are slowing your thinking down and possibly use the example of your mind as a lake that I gave you in the beginning of the book.

Let me, if I may, give you another personal example of how I apply this in my own life. When my ex-wife and I moved to London from South Africa, we left behind all our friends, all our family, our jobs, and everything we love and care about. We left behind all our possessions, all the presents we got from our engagement and our wedding. Our entire social fabric was stripped away from us as we made the decision to emigrate. On the scale of stressful life events, I think emigration falls just under the death of a spouse as one of the most stressful life events that people can go through. I can attest to that because we went through it — not once, but twice in a period of two years! Considering all of the above, we have generally done very well in coping emotionally and mentally with the changes. One day in London I came down with the flu on a Sunday morning. I thought it would go quickly but it stayed with me for a few days. On the third day I was feeling really sick. Physically, my body was in revolt, saying that it would like the cheque and that it would like to get off the ride. My thoughts started to rumble, like the first signs of a thunderstorm on its way, and I started to think really negatively about moving to London. Everything I thought about seemed to be bleak and I started to feel down not only physically but mentally.

And that becomes a double whammy when it's in its full throes as I'm sure most of you will no doubt have experienced. Luckily, I quickly realised what was going on and what I was doing to myself and I made the mental decision — in fact, I actually said it out loud to myself — that I was not going to think about any important issues in my life. I said that I know that when I am physically down everything I think about will seem negative and hopeless. I reminded myself that as soon as I feel better physically, my thoughts would naturally become more upbeat and positive. I will start to see opportunities again instead of dead ends. As I made the realization, I immediately felt better because I remembered that I had felt this way many times before and that each time it never really reflected the reality of my life. Just the realization alone of what was going on and why I was feeling so bad and thinking so negatively was enough to bring me out of it.

So you see, you can change your mind. Even with such a simple tool as deciding to just stop for a while and take time out from thinking. Thinking is way overrated anyway!

Everybody's emotions work in cycles. There is nothing static about the world of human emotions. It is just so important to realize that you can't always be up and that even the most die hard fan of positive thinking will tell you that there will be times in his life where his emotions are running the show and no amount of thinking will get them off center stage. We need to be able to ride the tide. You don't have to enjoy the ride — just like some people don't enjoy a roller-coaster ride —but at least realize that the ride will come to an end and that your emotions will come back up again. Maybe not in the next hour, maybe not in the next day, but they *will* come back up again and you will carry on and things will be all right. Remember:

"This Too Shall Pass"

CHAPTER 5 — THE SUBCONSCIOUS WAY TO CHANGE YOUR MIND AND YOUR LIFE

There is no doubt in my mind that there is immense power in visualising what you want to happen in your life. When I first heard about the concept that you can actually create your own reality, I thought it was a nice idea and thought "Wouldn't it be nice if that were true?" However, I never really thought it would work and whenever I tried to use any of the techniques for visualising what I wanted, I would think it was nice to picture but it probably wouldn't do any good. I mean, how could a simple action like picturing something in my mind lead to actual physical, cosmic and concrete changes in my everyday reality? How could I just picture what I wanted and then make it appear in reality? We don't live in a world where "magic" is real! Do we?

One might say that what we call "magic" could actually be a process of creation that we do not understand, and that once we do understand that process of creation it becomes nothing more than an everyday reality in our lives, which we accept without questioning. If you brought somebody out of the 1700s and showed them an airplane flying through the sky they would no doubt gasp and gawk in disbelief and then turn to calling it "magic" because they would have no way of understanding how the process of flight works. They would have no understanding of the *laws* of aerodynamics that allow a huge hunk of incredibly heavy machinery to fly through the air as if it weighed nothing more than a feather! But the laws operate independent of our knowledge of them. I believe that there are spiritual laws that operate in our universe in much the same way that we have physical laws. Some laws work for you whether you know about them or not, such as the law of gravity. Other laws you need to understand and use in the correct way for them to work to your advantage and for you to achieve your desired outcome. The laws of visualization and manifestation of what you would like to see happen in your life are part of those unseen laws that you can learn to work with as you begin to understand them better.

After a while of using these techniques, and admittedly, even then I really did very little to try to really picture what I wanted, I started to notice things happening. As an example, when I was still studying towards my degree at university, my first car was a little red Mini. As cute as it was to drive, I really didn't feel very good driving it through the campus parking lot and seeing how many other students were driving cars better than mine (which wasn't hard to achieve). Besides the issue of the status that I was so worried about at the age of 19, the car also gave me endless trouble. The driver's door was hanging onto its hinges for dear life and I was often worried I would be driving along and suddenly feel a gust of wind rush through the car as the door fell clean off onto the concrete highway! The car often had oil and brake problems (among countless others) and so, admittedly, I really didn't want the car anymore. The problem was, I was still a 19-year-old student with practically no money and my parents weren't in a financial state to be able to do anything about getting me a better car.

I really wanted something else but just didn't see how it would ever happen.

One day as I was driving the car to university I felt so despondent about the situation, I wanted to scream but instead I surprised myself by saying out loud that I *accept* the situation as it is. I said to myself that I understood that it was just the way things had to be for now but that things would soon change. I would get another car and feel a lot better about going to pick up a girl for a date in my new car rather than my Mini (which for all intents and purposes could have been a bicycle in my eyes when it came to picking up women for dates).

Once I had accepted the current situation, I decided that I would make a concerted effort to try to visualise what I wanted. I thought that I actually had nothing to lose by spending a few minutes each day picturing what it would be like to be driving a different car and what that car would look like.

I started to get specific and eventually came to focus my attention on the VW Citi Golf. Every time I saw one, especially a blue one, on the road I would look at it and record the picture of it in my mind. I started to imagine what it would feel like to be behind the wheel of the car, the black leather seats, and the dashboard at night. I imagined how I would feel driving the car through the campus parking lot.

After about a month of doing this, I got a call from a friend of mine who was working for his uncle's used car lot. He told me that he had just got in a blue Citi Golf with black leather seats and that he was thinking of buying it for himself.

I immediately told him I wanted to see the car. I had never told him that I even wanted a car, never mind that I was looking for a blue Citi Golf. I didn't even know how I could ever possibly buy the car, but I wanted to see it. So he took the car home that evening and came past our house. My father came out with me to see the car and liked it too. As soon as I saw the car come down the driveway of our house I knew this car would be mine. I had willed it and imagined it into my life. Needless to say, things sort of fell into place after that. We sold my Mini to a guy who worked for my father and my father sold his old motorbike and we got the blue Citi Golf. I was absolutely exhilarated and amazed at what had happened. I remember driving around in my Citi Golf feeling like a "new" man.

Even after that I didn't *really* take visualization seriously. I thought: "I suppose it's possible but it's more likely that this was a *coincidence* and it might have happened on its own anyway."

Having said that, I started to experiment with visualization and guided imagery. Guided imagery is a process used to work directly with the subconscious mind by giving it images and thoughts that you want to be true in your life. It is done in a semi-hypnotic state and can be used by anyone as it is very easy to do even by yourself. I will explain a little later how you can do this.

After the car situation, the next time I remember using creative visualization was when I wanted to move out of home and get my own apartment. When I first began to think about moving out, it was quite a stretch for me to imagine what it would be like to be on my own (or with a partner) in my own place. You can always tell how far you have to go and how much effort you need to put into visualising by the amount of resistance you feel when you try to picture what you want. The more resistance your mind gives you to what you are trying to picture or visualise, the more times you should visualise what you want until it becomes comfortable for you and easy to picture. I remember that each time I visualised the place I was going to live in, I would add more detail to what it looked like. I imagined that it was in a complex. In South Africa, it is much safer to live in a security-guarded complex due to the number of car hijackings that occur outside people's houses. Anyhow, the complex looked newly built, our (my imaginary future girlfriend or wife and myself) apartment was on the top level and I imagined myself walking up a flight of stairs on the outside of the building to get to our door. I imagined what the living room and kitchen would look like. When I imagined the living room area, my mind added in a detail that I cannot consciously remember putting in myself. It was a balcony. I imagined a breeze blowing the curtains back and the feeling of the cool air on my skin. I also imagined sitting in a chair on the balcony having a glass of wine and enjoying the view. I think I visualised this place over half a dozen times. Each time with more detail. I also imagined it to be in a suburb, Dowerglen that I had always wanted to live in.

About a year later, I had just come back from a trip to London and was now looking for a place for my new fiancé and myself to live in. It was a Saturday morning and my friend Alan was going to help me look through the classifieds and go and look at a few places. The first thing I noticed was an advertisement for an apartment in the area that I had imagined living in — Dowerglen. The price was in my range, which was also unusual for Dowerglen, as it is quite an expensive area to live in. I called the number and the guy on the other line said that it was still available but that I had better hurry and get over there because it would go fast. We jumped into my car and drove to the complex.

It was about two blocks away from where I had visualised living. The complex was absolutely beautiful, clean, and looked like it had been newly built. We drove around to the number he had given us. I got out the car and looked to see where number 35 was. It was at the top of a flight of outside stairs. We went up and I immediately knew I wanted it. It had a huge balcony and a view of Johannesburg that was just amazing. The sliding doors to the balcony were open and the curtains were blowing in the gentle breeze. I didn't have much time to make up my mind, but I didn't need to. I loved it and I told the guy I would take it.

The funny thing is, I only remembered what I had visualised about three months after we had moved in and only then did I realize how many of the details of what I had visualised had come true. I was absolutely amazed when I realised how powerful the visualization had been and that there could be no doubts that the guided imagery that I used had created this as a reality for me. I was thrilled!

What I have suggested to you about how to get things in life is not a new concept and yet very few people know about it or use it to get what they need or want. The concept that I am speaking about has been put forward by many writers and influential minds in the past in some form or another. Some have said it is a way of visualization, others have said that it is a religious certitude but the basic premise is this:

The best way to get something is to already have it.

I can almost see the smirk on your face and you're probably thinking, "What the heck is this fool on about?" I know it sounds a bit ridiculous, I mean, if you don't have something you can't already have it, right? Well, let's look at this a bit closer:

When you don't have something and you really feel that you need or want that thing desperately and you're not getting it, how does that make you feel? It makes you feel anxious, it upsets you and you "charge" everything around you with a negative energy of lack and need. Nine times out of ten, this attitude will tend to push what you want even farther away from you. However, how much easier do you think it is to get something once you already have it? And by "having it," I don't necessarily mean having it in concrete objective reality. You can close your eyes and see yourself having something in an instant. What do you think seeing yourself already in possession of the thing you desire will do to your motivation and your feelings of confidence and faith? I'll let you decide.

This seemingly illogical concept of already having something before you get it can be illustrated in many varied life situations. Consider the following example:

> Gary is a single guy who is looking for a partner. He is very desperate to find someone and it shows every time he approaches a woman for a date. Each time he approaches a prospective partner he is anxious because he feels that all his hopes are riding on her. He thus puts a lot of pressure on himself and acts nervous and needy. His response rate is thus dismally low and as he gets rejected each time his self-esteem gets lower and lower and he starts to actualize his initial subjective feelings of lack into objective reality. Gary also starts to *visualise* himself failing each time he makes an attempt and that visualization starts to become his reality. He is getting himself caught in the trap of using his past failures as references for his future endeavors. What he should really be doing is picturing and visualising success no matter what, because with a positive visualization of success will come confidence, self esteem and the actual ability to get that date!

> Alan is also a single guy who is looking for a partner. His **belief** is that there is an abundance of women in the world. There are hundreds and thousands of women who live just in his city not to mention how many live in his country. Alan thinks that with such abundance around him, the chances of him finding a woman, or better yet a woman finding

him, are pretty good. He thus approaches each prospective partner with the **feeling** that it is a matter of time before he finds someone and thus he **believes**, in his subconscious and conscious minds, that he already has what he wants. He thus feels confident and radiates that confidence outwards. He can actually **see himself** being successful. He can see himself enjoying going out with a woman, having fun and sharing intimate moments. The women that he dates can sense that he is not desperate and that intrigues them, so they feel more attracted to him. Nobody is attracted to desperation, most everybody is attracted to confidence and a good self esteem and so Alan soon finds that he has what he already believed he possessed. His visualization has become his reality.

The same concept works when one is looking for a job. It is always easier to find a job when one is already in one. If you aren't happy in your current position and you feel like you need a change for the better, you are in a win-win situation in terms of improving your life. This is because you already have the security of having an income and a job to go to each day but at the same time you are free to keep your options open and look out for a better job. Without a feeling of desperation that one would feel when unemployed, your chances are much improved in an interview because the employer will sense that you are not desperate for the job and this will be intriguing.

I am not saying that this only works for those who are employed. As I described earlier, you don't necessarily have to have the thing you want in objective reality. If you can impose on your mind a picture of yourself already in a position, even if you are unemployed temporarily, the chances are that you will conduct yourself far better and with much less anxiety in a job interview. Act as if you are employed, and I assure you that your chances of becoming employed will increase accordingly!

Following is a 10-step process you can use if you want to do guided imagery or creative visualization to help you get something, change something or improve something in your life.

1. Find a spot where you can relax and where you won't be disturbed by a telephone or any other distractions. It could be on your bed, on your couch or even outside on a comfortable chair. You can do this either sitting up or lying down, whichever is more comfortable for you.

2. Loosen any bit of clothing that may be too tight or may feel restricting on your body.

3. Close your eyes and begin to concentrate on your breathing and your body. Your breathing is the most crucial aspect of your physiology that you need to be focused on in the beginning stages of relaxing your mind and body for creative visualization.

4. Take a deep breath in through your nose, push the air down into your solar plexus, near your stomach, and then breathe it out noisily through your mouth. You should feel your stomach move outward and bulge a bit as the air pushes your diaphragm further down. You may find that the first time you try to do this, your lungs don't seem to take in much air. You may feel restricted, however, once you continue to do further breaths in and out you will find the muscles relaxing and you will steadily be able to bring in bigger and bigger amounts of air with more ease.

5. Once you start to feel your body relaxing, start to focus on your feet. Imagine that a white or blue light is moving along your body, starting at your feet, and everywhere it goes it relaxes your muscles, tendons and joints. Move the light from your feet to your ankles, from your ankles to your calves, knees, thighs and hips. Continue on like this through the rest of your body and each time you think of a part of your body and imagine that white

light moving over it, *feel* that part release its tension and let go. *Feel* it relax and become loose and flowing. Once you have been through your body once, go through it with another quick mental check, noticing where there may still be some tension and mentally and physically letting that tension or anxiety go.

6. You should now feel very relaxed. Now you can start moving your mind into a deeper state of relaxation by using the analogy of yourself walking down or up a 10-step staircase. With each step that you take, you start to feel more and more relaxed. You can feel your body either becoming more and more heavy or more and more light as you move onto the next step.

7. When you get to the very top or bottom of the stairs you should imagine yourself in an environment that you love. This can be a beautiful garden; standing on the beach looking at the waves crashing on the shore; standing on top of a mountain or even in your own comfortable living room. Anywhere that makes you feel safe, secure, and at peace. Spend some time in this place, seeing your surroundings, feeling the physical sensations of that place, hearing the sounds, smelling the aromas or scents, and touching the physical objects or elements that are surrounding you.

8. After about five minutes, you can clear that picture and begin to imagine, paint a picture, or play a movie of the thing you most want to create or change in your life. You may want to bring something into your life or you may want to move something out of your life. You may want to start doing something or you may want to stop doing something. Whatever it is, begin to imagine the thing you want. Use all your senses in bringing the image or images to light. See yourself doing, being, having, using, and enjoying what you really want. Expand on your picture or visualization. Move around

inside your new reality, see all the characteristics of the thing, person, or event that you want to attract or to happen in your life. The best part about this process is that it is fun and unbound by the laws of reality as it stands now. You are free to imagine anything your mind is capable of imagining. Do not worry if you think you are not good at imagining, just try, and even pretend that you can. It will be fine. Just relax into it.

9. A crucial element to this exercise is for you to start to feel the emotions that this visualization is creating for you. Now, hopefully you will be feeling wonderful emotions such as joy, happiness, and excitement. If what you are picturing is not bringing in any of those feelings then you may not be picturing something that you really want and that means a lot to you. The reason I say you need the emotional feeling of actually being there or having that item or becoming that person, is because the more you create the feelings inside your mind and body, the more you are reaching the essential part of yourself that can and will make it happen — your subconscious mind. When you imagine with emotional intensity you are speaking the language of your subconscious mind and it will respond to your thoughts and your emotion by helping you create the reality you have imagined. This is part of the process of working with the unseen law of creative visualization.

10. After you have achieved some level of emotional intensity, you can then let the image go and imagine yourself back at the staircase. Start to climb either up or down the stairs from 10 to 1 or 1 to 10 (depending on which way you went up or down before!), and with each step you can feel yourself becoming more and more awake. Start to notice different parts of your body, becoming aware of the ground, chair or bed beneath you. Start to feel your breathing returning to normal and imagine that every living cell in your body is returning to perfect,

healthy functioning. Start to become more and more alert and awake as you near the end of the staircase and when you reach either the top or the bottom you can open your eyes.

What you will find (if you have done this process properly and have reach a fairly good level of relaxation) is that you may very well have a good long stretch when you wake up as if you had just had the most refreshing sleep for a few hours. If you do feel this way, that is a sure sign that you have reached deep down into your subconscious mind and that you are making excellent progress in your journey to changing your mind and changing your life!

Sleeping on the Job! Using Guided Meditation Tapes

There are some excellent tapes that can be used to do guided meditation or visualization at night while you are asleep. When we sleep, our conscious mind fades into the background in the same manner that it does when one is under hypnosis. You are more able to reach the subconscious mind at these times. It is very difficult to try and do your own guided visualization when you are about to fall asleep because that's exactly what you will do — fall asleep.

Besides being an excellent way for you to reach your subconscious mind and tell it what you want, they are also very good at helping you relax.

These tapes will often have a particular topic, such as increasing abundance, reducing stress, or healing your body and we have found them to be very beneficial. To give you one example, a number of years ago, my ex-wife and I decided that we wanted to start to change our thoughts and beliefs about money. We had both grown up in households where money was tight and as a result had fairly strong scarcity beliefs about money. Although I did consciously work at trying to believe that my situation would change, my outer reality was only reflecting a life of scarcity and lack of abundance. I had quite a few debts, including credit card debt, a student loan I was still slowly repaying, and a car loan that was only about half paid off. I also owed some family some money that I had borrowed from them, and various other clothing accounts and medical bills. From the age of 20, when I first took on the student loan, I had never been in the clear and was very concerned about how I would ever get out of the little mountain of debt that I owed. I was also feeling under immense strain and was having to deal with quite a bit of guilt over not being able to pay my family back their money.

I realised that I obviously had some negative, subconscious beliefs about money and abundance that needed to be changed before anything in my outer reality would change. So we decided that although we were a little sceptical about the effects that listening to tapes would have on us while we slept, we thought we had nothing to lose. After listening to one of the tapes while we were awake, we felt that it was a really nice tape and that it couldn't do us any harm. At the least, we would get a good night's sleep and wake up feeling pretty refreshed!

We started playing a tape on abundance every single night as we went to sleep for about a six month period. The tape dealt with negative beliefs or scripts that we might have had about money. It made us affirm to our subconscious mind that we desired more abundance, that we deserved more abundance, and that more abundance was entering our reality. The results were amazing. Now, you can choose to say to yourself when you hear these "results," that it was all a coincidence and that what followed was going to happen anyway and we have no way of proving that it was the tapes that created the results. You could say that, yes, and indeed, we even thought that ourselves a few times. But as our reality continued to change and the results just kept coming at us in bigger and bigger proportions, we found it very hard to believe that it *wasn't* the subconscious programming. Abundance kept pouring into our lives, which eventually led to me getting rid of all the debt I owed and us having enough money to buy two return tickets to Australia and to London at the same time. One of the things that occurred just before we emigrated was that the managing director of the company I worked for said that if I could finish the project I was working on before we left he would give me a bonus. I didn't know what the bonus would be, but it ended up being a double cheque. We also managed to get everything we needed to emigrate to the UK and had enough left over for us to be able to cope in pounds with our very weak South African rands for a few months living expenses. We have not only used this powerful method of changing your life for abundance, but also for health, creating peace and calm in our lives, and many other issues that we wanted to change in our subconscious minds so that we could find it easier to change our conscious reality.

How does this process work?

This process of visualising what you want is also linked to a universal law or truth that we bring to ourselves what we believe we can have. Through the process of visualization and imprinting on the subconscious mind a picture or an intention of what we want, we are making ourselves clear to the universe and the universe will respond to us. Once again we need to be aware of what we are doing, because we can just as easily attract negative events, people, and experiences into our lives if that is what we choose to focus on. Just as your subconscious mind will listen to what you tell it is true, the universe will bring to you what you continuously focus on and picture in your mind. If you do a survey of some of the most successful people in the world who have achieved amazing results in their lives, you will find that they have all used the process of visualising what they want in one form or another. I could name Jim Carrey, Steven Spielberg, and Oprah Winfrey just to start.

I highly recommend you look into the amazingly powerful process of visualization. It really cannot do you any harm if you picture positive and successful outcomes for your life. If you link your visualizations to a higher cause of helping others, even better!

If you think about it, everything you see around you right now, besides nature itself, is man made and had to have its beginning in someone's mind. Someone had to visualise what that chair was going to look like that you are now sitting on. Someone had to imagine a device that could cool down food and invented the fridge — but first it would have been a thought in their mind and a picture in their mind's eye about what they wanted to achieve! From the tallest skyscrapers to the little kennel your dog sleeps in, they all had to be imagined and thought of by someone before they came into being. That same power of thought, imagination and creation is available to all of us and is not the province of only a select few. This means that you can create anything you want in your life because you have the ability to think, imagine, visualise, and take action. And if you do these things consistently and with enough commitment, you are going to achieve your goal and create whatever you want in your life.

When you first start to visualise you may find that your mind tries to resist what you are trying to picture. If you find this happening that is a good sign that you need to intensify the amount of time you are spending visualising what you want, because your subconscious mind is resisting that image. This may be because deep down you don't feel you can have it or you may feel you are not good enough or smart enough to get there and achieve what you want. You need to impress upon your mind that you can and will have the things you are picturing and the more you picture it, the easier you will find it becomes and each time you will find yourself adding in more detail to the picture until it becomes almost a reality for you. When you are at that point, you are getting very close to creating what you want. If you keep at it, you will see that it will happen for you just as you have imagined it.

Your mind gives you the ability to visualise and see a better, more successful and happy future for yourself. You have the choice to picture whatever you want no matter how things are going for you right now. Why not choose to see your life working the way you want? It's a very powerful tool to change your life...use it!

CHAPTER 6 — GOAL SETTING!

Goal setting is a tremendously under-utilized tool for change and growth in our lives. So few people do it and even less people really understand how effective it can be. I truly believe in the power of goal setting, as I have seen the results it can achieve in my own life as well as in the lives of others. There have even been times in my life where I have set goals that I didn't believe I could ever achieve, but I set them anyway and I have found myself being amazed time and time again when I look back over the goals that I have written in my goal book, at how many ticks I can place next to goals that have been achieved. What I would like to do in this chapter is explain some of the essential things you need to do in order to set effective goals, monitor those goals and take action towards their achievement. Then I would like to give you some examples from my own experience to show you how effective goal setting can be, especially when it is done in conjunction with the visualization and imagery techniques I discussed in the previous chapter. If you can discipline yourself to do both (goal setting and visualising what you want), you will have a dynamite method for achieving real change in your life and for achieving some of your most cherished dreams and desires.

Many writers and motivational speakers have said that it is important to **write your goals down.** I believe this is very true and is one of the key elements in achieving what you want. There is no doubt a mysterious process at work when one commits oneself to achieving something in black and white. What you are doing is bringing something out of the ethereal world of your mind and thoughts into the real and tangible world of your life. You are making the unmanifest manifest and the unseen seen. When you state quite clearly to the universe what it is you would like to achieve, there is nothing wishy-washy about it anymore. You have taken the time to define something that the universe can work with. A good analogy is that of an airplane taking off for a destination that it hasn't quite yet defined, but which it would really like to get to! Would you like to be onboard that airplane? I wouldn't. I would much prefer that the captain has decided on his destination (hopefully the same destination I want to get to) and that he has plotted a course on how he is going to get there. This is an example, albeit on a smaller scale, of the process of goal setting.

So, the first step is to bring it out of the invisible world of thought, assumption, hopes and desires and bring it into the world of concrete reality, pen and paper, step and process.

Goal setting is not complicated and don't let anyone ever tell you otherwise. It is not hard and it does not have to seem like a lot of effort and wasted time. Believe me when I tell you it is not wasted time. The best thing about putting your goals down on paper is that it costs you nothing and you don't even have to believe it will work for it to actually work! If you will just take some time to sit down and do it, you will be doing yourself a gigantic favour and you will soon be amazed at the results you can consistently achieve. I have often come across people who fear goal setting. People, for one reason or another, would rather run away from the concept of goal setting because it strikes a chord of fear in them that they probably couldn't explain if they tried. They just prefer to keep their most cherished dreams and desires safe away from the possibility of being faced with what they would actually have to do to achieve what they want. They would rather hope and wish that what they want to achieve would happen purely by coincidence, luck or chance. Now, the funny thing is, your goals may very well come about through a mixture of what seem like coincidences, luck and chance, but I can almost assure you that if you haven't even tried to commit your goals to writing, it is unlikely this will ever happen. It is true that people seem to achieve goals sometimes through such things as chance and coincidence, but I am pretty much willing to bet they had it written down first. There's the possibility that the people who shy away from goal setting — whether it's to lose weight or to achieve fame and fortune — are to some extent afraid of failing. Let's face it, most of us are afraid of failing, but all we need to do to change this is to learn how to perceive what happens in a different light. As I mentioned before, Tony Robbins explains the concept that we need to entrench a new belief system, which includes the idea of not believing in failure and that all we ever do is achieve a certain set of results. If we don't like the results, all we really need to do to get new results is change what we are doing, what we are thinking, and what our beliefs or perceptions are. Sometimes people can achieve their goals without even realizing it. They may for instance have decided a few years ago that they would like to reach a certain level of wealth in their lives. Once they reached that level, they don't even go back to their goals and tick it off the list. They just automatically want a higher level of wealth and therefore don't feel like they have achieved what they set out to achieve. All it would take is a mental readjustment to see that they are successful and that they have the ability to achieve their goals in life, one step at a time. I will talk more about recognizing your successes in life in a later chapter.

Some Examples

When I was still at the university, nearing the end of my third year, I was not sure how I was ever going to become a psychologist. The reason is that I had already taken out loans for my undergraduate degree and I was not sure how I would ever pay for my honours degree and my master's degree. I also wasn't sure whether I would even get into the courses because I knew that they only took about 20 people each year out of hundreds of students who applied. I had already been setting goals in my life for a few years with some good results and I realised that I needed to set some goals with regards to becoming a psychologist. I knew that besides needing the money to study and getting into the courses, I would then need to get an internship at a company for a year before I would qualify as a psychologist. I was also concerned that if I had to continue my loans with the bank for another two years I would end up owing so much money when I graduated that I just couldn't see how I would pay it all back. I didn't want to be stuck with loans that I would need to pay off for the rest of my life!

This task seemed very daunting and almost like a dream at that stage of my life and I thought that I would probably only get to do my masters degree later in my twenties and I would have to do it part time whilst I was working. Having thought about that, I knew that it was one of my great life goals at that stage to qualify as a psychologist and it was something I really wanted to achieve so I knew I had to take the next step, which was to commit it to paper and to set a time line for when I wanted to achieve it by. So, I took out my old goal book (which is a hardcover A5 booklet that I still have with me today) and I wrote down the following three-year goal (I am giving this to you directly from my goal book) :

3 Year Plan

Age Now: 21, year 1997

1998:

1. I will do my honours degree in Psychology through either RAU, WITS or UNISA

1999:

1. Get a job as either a human resources or personnel manager. Something to do with psychology in organisations.
2. Maybe study Masters Degree part-time through UNISA

2000:

1. Start earning a decent salary and begin to pay back loans to the bank as fast as possible!
2. Start or complete Masters Degree

Now, I would be the first to say that I didn't exactly follow the best practice in writing down those goals and I have, since then, learned to be much more direct and specific. However, regardless of that, this is what actually happened in the years after I set that goal.

1998:

I got into the honours degree in psychology. When I applied I was also told that I could apply for a scholarship as I had achieved certain marks for my undergrad degree that allowed me to enter (I hadn't even heard of this before). If I got the post-merit award, I would not have to pay for my studies, but I would have to work for the psychology department by tutoring second year students, which I was happy to do. I was awarded the post-merit scholarship and therefore didn't need to keep borrowing money from the bank and, in fact, I actually got paid some money for tutoring the second-year students in statistics and research design — what a bonus!

1999:

I got into the master's course with a fair amount of ease — although I had to work very hard during my honours year to ensure I kept my marks at the right levels. This was a true surprise for me as I had really thought I would only get to do my master's later on in life and that I would need to study it part-time due to money constraints. I was once again awarded the post-merit award and worked for the department by marking first year psychology essays for which I was once again paid some nice pocket money.

2000:

I started my internship at a growing financial technology company and after a year I qualified as a psychologist and was promoted to human resources manager.

I do not show you these goals to impress you or anything like that. All I want you to see is that even though I may not have couched my goals in the best possible way (I will show you a better way a little later on), my goals were still achieved, often ahead of my wildest expectations and in ways that I could not have predicted. I got help from unexpected sources because I had defined to the universe what I wanted to achieve, and the universe helped me to get there in the easiest possible way. This is just one example of the many examples I could give you of goals coming to life and being achieved. I have also helped others to set goals and have seen the same type of results. I find that the saying "be careful what you wish for because you just might get it" is 100 times stronger when you actually sit down and write out your goals. If you set them, they will happen, sometimes not quite in the time frame you have given, but almost certainly they will happen — provided they are the right goals for you and the universe concurs with what you want to achieve.

Let us now go back to how we actually begin to set our goals. Here is a simple, easy to follow process that you can use to set any goal you want to in your life:

1. First decide what it is you would like to achieve. In doing this you need to be able to mix a certain amount of realism with a major dash of dreams and desires. I would call the combination of the two "dreamism." Think about your goal, decide if it is the right goal to set for yourself because it fits in with where you would like to see your life going and it fits in with your values. For example, if one of your values is to have a nice family life, bring up a few kids and enjoy having friends and family around you all the time, then setting a goal to be a famous rock musician who tours the world all the time does not really fit in with your other values. This is not to say that being a famous rock musician you couldn't still have a great family life, it is just saying that it is less likely you would be able to spend as much time with your family as you would like. If you decide on something you want to achieve, something you want to change in your life and after checking that it does in fact fit in with your other values, then it is time to commit your goal to paper. This is the first step in bringing your goal to life and making it happen.

2. Take out a blank piece of paper and a pen and begin to write what it is you would like to change or create in

your life. Ensure that you frame the goal with the use of positive wording, for instance, if you want to lose weight, do not write "I don't want to be fat anymore," that is not going to motivate you or create the desired outcome. Goals should be set in the affirmative, for instance, "I will be thin and sexy." Much better!

3. Next, write out exactly why it is you want to achieve this goal. Why is it so important for you to achieve? What do you think the benefits will be to you, your family and friends, your community?

4. Continue to write out all the major goals that you have for yourself. This is the time that you must not let reality block you from coming up with outrageous goals, always use this formula when you are creating inspiring life goals: "If I had no limits to my time, financial resources or ability, what would I like to become, start doing, or achieve in my life?" You may also want to imagine yourself at 85 looking back on your life with joy and pride. What are the things you would have accomplished? What contribution would you have made to society? How will people remember you and who will remember you?

5. Now you should write down a time frame in which you would like to achieve these goals. Do you think you could achieve them in two years? Five years? Ten years? Write down how old you will be when you achieve your goal. Once you have written down the time frames for each of your goals, order them in the sequence from the earliest time frame to the longest

6. Now, looking at your goals that are in the closest proximity to where you are now, for instance, the goals you want to achieve in the next three to five years. Take each one and break it down into smaller chunks that you can take action on in the next year. These will become your one year, short-term goals.

7. Don't worry about how you are going to achieve the broader and more distant goals. It is an immutable law of goal setting that once the goal is set, it will create circumstances, people and events in your life that will help you achieve it. Once set, it is imperative that you do not become a slave to the goal or worry so much about whether you are going to achieve it or not. If it is the right goal for you and it is in God's master plan then you will achieve it, no doubt. I have seen it time and again, when I have gone back over goals that I wrote down years ago. I never knew at the time how I could achieve them and I never could foresee how certain people would come into my life at just the right time, or events would happen that pushed me in the direction suitable for achieving written goals. I have constantly been amazed when going back over these goal lists at how many of the goals were achieved; and not only that but also achieved according to the timeline set! It's almost freaky but it works, and why not use something that works in helping you achieve what you want out of life? It is an act of creation to bring your desires and thoughts into reality by committing them to paper. I believe that it is this act that starts the ball rolling and gets your life moving in the direction you desire.

8. Review your goals at least once a year but preferably every six months to see how you are doing. You may find that one of your one-year goals has already been achieved or you might notice that your aims have changed and you can then modify your goals. There is nothing like going back to a goal list each year to renew your commitment to achieving something, especially when you see that you are achieving things you never dreamed possible. Remember to also give yourself some easy goals to achieve to help you get the momentum going. There is nothing like a little success to help you get motivated to go for the bigger challenges! Go for it and good luck!

CHAPTER 7 — MEDITATION

What can I say about meditation that hasn't already been said in the hundreds of other books about the subject? Well, I think what I can describe for you is my own experimenting and experience with meditation and why I think it is so useful as a tool to change your mind.

If meditation is new to you, as it would be for many people, you may feel that it is something that is very "out there" and esoteric. Maybe you feel that only funny people wearing coloured sashes or gowns should meditate? I must admit that when I first thought of meditation I thought it was a useful way to fall asleep at best and at worst a bloody waste of time! The thing about it is this: meditation actually works! 100 percent of the time. It costs you absolutely nothing. No therapists to pay large sums of money (I include myself in that!), no exercise and diet guru and no endless soul searching to find some peace and calm. There is very little we actually know about the physical mechanisms behind meditation or what actually happens when you do it. There is, however, more and more research happening as science develops ever more sophisticated methods of seeing what happens in our brains when certain events take place when we are undergoing various exercises or thought processes. I read in a recent article that scientists have done studies on the actual chemical changes that seem to occur in the brain when someone meditates. It seems quite extraordinary that something as simple as keeping your mind calm and clear for a ten to twenty minute period can have profound effects on your mood by actually physically altering the chemistry in your brain. We know that hard physical exercise releases endorphins in the brain that make us feel relaxed and positive. Similar processes happen when we meditate.

What do we mean by the word meditate? When I think of the sound of that word it reminds me of the word levitate, so I have this picture of someone sitting cross legged and hovering a few feet off the ground! Well, obviously that is not what we mean and if you can do something like that, then good on you! What I mean when I talk about meditating is the process of clearing out the thoughts that are running around in your mind. I'm willing to make a little bet that there have been times in your life when you have found yourself thinking so much during the day that you felt like your head was spinning. You may also have felt like your head was just bursting with so many thoughts and ideas going backwards and forwards that you literally felt like your mind was on a treadmill that you couldn't get off of. Some people will feel like they need to sleep to get their minds to calm down. This is not always a solution though. The reason is that your subconscious mind will take over and continue to try and sort the issues out. Try and "think" things through and you may just end up having a very restless sleep.

When you meditate, you are still fully conscious and aware of what's happening around you and especially inside your mind and body. When you sit down and get quiet you will often realize how noisy things are inside your mind.

Let there be no illusions about this from the start — it isn't easy to meditate, especially when you are new at it. Your mind will be like an untrained puppy, smelling around and then bolting off in a different direction when it gets a scent of something interesting to pursue. You will need to take your mind to obedience classes. There is no doubt in my mind that many people who try meditate find that they cannot control or calm down their thoughts for long enough to actually feel the benefits of what I am talking about. You might sit down, go through the process I am going to describe and after twenty minutes or even half an hour still feel erratic and agitated. You may decide at that point that this doesn't work, but I implore you to keep trying. The most important thing to remember when you try to relax your mind for the first time is that it is actually very new for your mind. It is the same as when you first learned to ride a bike or swim. You started out slowly and you probably didn't get it right the first few times but you knew that people learned how to ride and swim after a little bit of effort and practice and you wanted to learn too and feel what it is like to be proficient at it and reap the rewards! So, too, with meditating. Each time you sit down and get quiet, whether it's for ten minutes or thirty minutes, it will help you to get better and better at it. You will also find that each time you do it your mind will cooperate more quickly and effectively to the point that you can eventually get yourself into a calm state of mind and reap the benefits in a few minutes.

One of they key benefits you *will* receive from meditating is becoming calmer, more focused in your thinking and often feeling a much-needed sense of peace and joy. You will find that after a session of keeping your mind and body still, your thoughts naturally become more positive. You will feel renewed and refreshed to continue whatever activity you may have been busy with before you started. I always advocate meditating or doing exercise in the early evening after work or study. It gives your mind and body a much needed rest and then revitalises you for the evening. This is very helpful when one needs to either work or study at night or run a home with kids!

I don't believe that there is any one technique for meditation. It is a personal experience that you will create for yourself and through which you will learn your own specific techniques to get the best out of the process. However, I would offer the following guidelines based on my experience:

1. Find a comfortable spot where you will not be disturbed by noise or anything else that may distract you from keeping still and quiet. Make sure you are warm, because when you begin to meditate you will probably find that your body temperature will drop slightly as you conserve energy and slow everything down.

2. Get yourself into a comfortable position. I prefer to keep my legs crossed in front of me, as I find this helps me to keep my back straight and keep me in a sitting position. It is okay to do this on your bed, however I must emphasize that you may be tempted to lie flat, in which case you will probably just nod off to sleep! You have also programmed yourself to associate lying on your bed with going to sleep, so it's probably best to go for a comfortable spot on the carpet or on a couch.

3. It is essential that at least your upper back and head are upright. This helps to ensure that you stay awake and aware during the meditation. If you nod off to sleep, you will not get the benefits I am talking about here. Only when you have calmed your mind down enough and still remain aware of your body and thoughts will you begin to feel what it is like to just relax and be there in the moment.

4. As mentioned in one of the earlier chapters of this book, you may want to picture your mind as a lake that starts off very wavy and bumpy and as you progressively relax and let each thought train go past, you see the waters of the lake getting calmer and calmer. You should continue to visualise this until you can see the water still and smooth and until you can see the mirror image on the surface of the lake. Possibly you might like to picture a still blue sky with clouds gently gliding by reflected in the calm stillness of the lake.

5. It is also essential that you regulate and focus on your breathing. You achieve two vital objectives when you do this:

    •   You bring more oxygen into your lungs and blood stream, which is very useful in helping you calm down your body and mind and feel more relaxed.

- You will find that by focusing on your breathing, you will be able to distract your mind from other thoughts that would have the potential to sidetrack your attempts to calm down and relax. If you would like a reminder of how to do your breathing, go back to page 62 where I showed you how to prepare yourself for guided imagery.

6. As you start to do this, you will notice, possibly for the first time in ages, how many thoughts are going on in your mind at one time. You will also notice where you are holding a clenched fist or where you have tightened your muscles or joints subconsciously. Take this time to do a mental inventory of your body and release any tension you may have.

7. To control your thoughts and begin to reduce their number, you will need to be very focused on letting thoughts come into your mind and then letting them go. It is also essential that you do not get upset or berate yourself when you find that you have spent the last five minutes of your meditation worrying about the presentation you have to do next week or what you are going to tell Aunt Jenny about why you can't make it to her tea party on Sunday! It's okay. When you catch yourself following a line of thought too far, just stop and let it go. Again, picture your mind as the sky and your thoughts like clouds going past. Rather than follow a cloud to see where its going, just focus on one spot in the sky and just let each cloud (thought) come into view and then move on, disappearing out of your vision.

8. Keep breathing deeply and calmly, keep releasing tension and keep letting your thoughts get fewer and quieter.

9. That's it! That's all you need to do!

I do not want to prescribe what I think your experience of meditation will be like. This is for you to experience and decide if it's something you want to continue with as a way of life. Don't make it regimented, like an exercise program, I really feel this is something you should go into at your own pace and use it whenever you feel the need for it. Obviously you will gain much greater benefit by doing it regularly, but this doesn't mean you have to.

My experience with meditating has been that even when I feel at my absolute worst, when I feel very negative and I feel like every thought is going on a wild rampage to make me feel miserable — meditation will always be able to reduce my levels of stress and tension. When my emotions are low and I don't feel like I'm coping or even if I am just feeling really stressed and agititated, I will make a point of doing a quiet meditation and without fail when I have spent at least twenty minutes doing it I will feel lighter, relieved, relaxed and more positive. If this is all you ever got out of doing meditation it would be worth it. Don't you think it's better to do twenty minutes of meditation to get the same results you would by popping a tranquilizer? I do. Why pay for pills when this is free and it is so much more beneficial? It's a natural high and if you get addicted to it that would be just fine!

When you start to become more proficient with meditation, you will also be able to start introducing some guided imagery at the end of the session of some visualization to attract something or someone into your life. To go from a meditative and relaxed state into a visualization is said to be more powerful than going directly into a visualization, because you will have already gotten yourself into a deeper and altered state of consciousness where you are already playing within the realms of your subconscious mind. When you then introduce pictures of something you want to achieve and see yourself achieving, having or doing those things, you create a powerful image that is sent out to the universe of what your desire is. This is an excellent way to attract something into your life. For a more detailed discussion on this you can refer back to the chapter on visualization and guided imagery.

Meditation has many benefits, some of which I have described above. What these should immediately indicate to you is the power of meditation and silent contemplation to help you change your experience of life. From stress to peace, from positive to negative, from doubt to certainty. See for yourself if what I am telling you is true or not. Go try it right now!

CHAPTER 8 — TAKING CONTROL
OF YOUR PHYSICAL LIFE

Although most people know that physical exercise is important for their health, few really comprehend just how important and vital it is for their psychological, emotional, financial, and spiritual health. The first and obvious reason one should exercise is because of the favorable effects it has on the body. It keeps the muscles toned and firm so that the body is able to move with greater ease and less effort, which in turn is less taxing on the heart. In getting the circulation going, physical exercise increases the general level of functioning of the body's organs and can actually lead to a boost in the functioning of the immune system. Exercise has also been shown to be effective in reducing incidences of cardio-vascular disease.

Thus, it is clear from a purely physical and biological standpoint that physical exercise is vital to healthy living and effective functioning. However, as mentioned, what most people don't realize is the effect that physical exercise has on emotions and psychological health. Many studies have been conducted on the beneficial effect that exercise has on levels of stress. It is believed that the primary reason is that physical exercise leads to the secretion of dopamine (which is a neurotransmitter in the brain associated with pleasure) that in turn reduces the levels of cognitive stress experienced by the person. It is also difficult for the mind to engage in stressful thinking when the body is undergoing a strenuous physical exercise routine.

This gives the mind a welcome respite against the continuous process of thoughts that have generally accumulated, especially where those thoughts have been negative and destructive.

In my own experience, I have found that going to a tae kwon do class has often helped me get through a number of difficult patches in my life. It has demonstrated to me time and time again the power of a heavy work out to destroy a negative thought pattern or mood-state. I studied tae kwon do for seven years. For most of that period I was studying for my psychology degree. I had an intensive period of two years when I did my honours and master's degrees right after one another. I was under immense pressure and I truly believe that if it weren't for the regular discipline of going to a tae kwon do class twice or three times a week, I would never have coped with all the stress.

One of the most important tricks in using this system of increasing one's mood-state and getting out of a negative thought pattern involves discipline. The reason is that most people, when caught in the throes of a powerful negative state or emotion, will tend to avoid their regular exercise regime because they "don't feel like it" or because of the energy used up by the stressful situation or negative state. They feel too "tired" to get up and go. The reason that I have put tired in quotation marks is because they are not usually physically tired, but mentally tired.

It is exactly at these points, when one is mentally tired and feeling like things are getting out of control (which often leads to increasing stress and discomfort) that one *must* head for the gym or get out those running shoes. I do need to add, however, that if the exercise itself is not sufficiently taxing and one is still able to think about one's life while doing the exercise, it is highly unlikely that it will have the desired effect. There should be a large amount of sweat involved and the more negative the mood-state, the more intense your exercise regime should be.

The so-called "tiredness" that one felt before the exercise usually dissipates and is replaced by a renewed feeling of energy and positive thought processes. It often feels as if a weight has been lifted and you may sometimes feel like a totally different person!

Generally, many people go to the gym or go for a run early in the morning. In terms of the kinds of benefits of physical exercise that I am talking about, going to the gym in the evening seems to me to be the better option. If one is already physically fit and is not experiencing any emotional or stressful problems then I see no reason why an early morning regime is problematic. However, if the majority of the stress that one experiences is caused by one's work or whatever thoughts one has had throughout the day, it becomes important (especially when one needs to keep energy levels high and thinking clear at night) to go for that exercise in the early evening. It gives one a mental break and physical "re-loading," which in turn leads to a mental "re-loading" of energy. In effect, it gives one a much needed "second wind," which can be very helpful if one needs to study at night or handle any number of activities pertaining to family or work after hours.

Lethargy breeds lethargy. I am sure you have had days when you feel lazy and you end up not doing much and lounging around the house. Aren't those the days you end up feeling incredibly tired and you wonder how it can be possible for you to have spent so much time "relaxing" and then feel so damn tired at the end of the day? On the other hand, I am sure you have also had days when you have been constantly on the go, even on weekends and you find that after doing so much you still feel pumped and ready for more. You have generated energy in your body through activity and your body has responded by giving you more energy. I bet you these are the days when your head hits the pillow at night and you are out for the count! And you end up having a good nights rest as well. Yes?

The movement of the body is a condition that many in our increasingly complex and "enhanced" society seem to ignore. It is one of the natural states of the human body to be in movement and to use the muscles and limbs to their fullest. The exhilaration one gets from running after having sat in a chair all day, or the feeling of being alive that one gets from using one's body and not only one's mind, lends itself to a balance which is essential for effective and healthy living. The benefits that result in terms of physical and mental efficiency, the increases in energy and the elevation of one's mood far outweigh the effort that is required for the organizing of the activity and the time and discipline needed to stick to a regime of physical exercise.

Even something like the simple act of going for a short walk around the block or to a park is incredibly beneficial to the human body, mind, and soul. I know that whenever I feel as if I am getting myself into a "thought-rut," I can decide to go for a walk or a bike ride to help dispel the negative thinking or mood that I am in. I have even gone and found somewhere where I can scream out my frustration or pound the ground with anger just so that I can let out all those negative and destructive emotions inside me. What you are doing is transferring that energy from a mental internal state to a physical external expression which helps you to release it from your mind and body. You may feel more physically tired afterwards, but you will definitely feel much better emotionally and your thinking will become clearer as well. As I have said before, sometimes you cannot think your way out of an emotional state, especially a deeply negative one, and it becomes important for you to allow thought to follow action and not the other way around. You need to get out there, find a park, or go look at the trees or anything that nature has to offer you.

If you are near the sea, you would be crazy not to use the powerful healing properties of the sea by going for a long walk along the beach, or even just looking at the waves and listening to the incredibly relaxing sounds. There is truly a power in nature to heal us. If you think about it, when you feel down or when you have had a really emotionally draining day, you literally feel how the life-force is sucked out of you. I have often found that the tiredness that comes from emotional upheaval is much more taxing and debilitating than the healthy tiredness one gets from a physically demanding day or event.

When we use physical energy, whether it's to exercise or for anything else, we usually get back more than we put in later on. I am sure you have experienced the second wind of energy after having gone for a run or to the gym. However, when it comes to emotional energy, it gets sapped much quicker and it affects you so much more when things in your life are draining you of mental and emotional energy. You may literally feel as if the life blood is running out of you and you feel lethargic, down, and sometimes unable to cope with life. It is at these times precisely that you need to get moving physically and get out into nature. Nature is alive with life force and energy. When you think about the ocean with its immense power and the constant flow of its waves; that's a lot of energy moving around out there! If you can go and stand on the edge of the shore and breathe in deeply and be still, you will feel that immense power and life force of the earth and it will help to renew the energy you have lost.

What I suggest is that you mentally open yourself up to receiving some of that energy into your body and most importantly, into your mind. If you don't have access to the sea, go find a park or a garden and sit down in it and quietly meditate. Listen to the sounds around you and breathe in gently. Again, visualise powerful healing and restoring energy filling your body and mind. You may want to picture a tank or empty battery and mentally see a vibrant and colourful liquid filling it up to the top. I have done this on many occasions and each time I walk away, I feel as if I have literally recharged my "batteries." The same incredible force that created everything in this universe — including you! — can be found everywhere in nature and you can make use of it as God intended. It is there for you and it is free. You don't have to pay for most of the best things in life so what have you got to lose? If nothing else, you will breathe in some fresh air, and even if you don't believe anything I have just written about life forces and energy, the physical and scientific facts are that when you breathe in correctly and deeply, your body begins to relax, the oxygen in your blood flows and you increase your levels of energy and begin to feel better.

If you are feeling stuck in a negative state and feel yourself spiralling further and further into a mental funk, get out of the house. Get out immediately and go somewhere. If it's for exercise, even better. But go out there and take some deep breaths and move your body.

Once the body is moving, you begin to breathe in more oxygen and your essential life force gets flowing again. The oxygen is carried by your blood to all the parts of your body and your whole system is stimulated into motion, energy creation and motivation. As everything begins to flow again, you will notice how the nature and flow of your thoughts will begin to change. The negative thoughts will be fewer and there just may be (and I'm pretty much betting there *will* be) some positive and motivating thoughts that will help you begin to feel better and start to think in a more rational and uplifting way.

At each moment we have a choice. Every time you feel down, you have a choice. You can lie there and say "what's the use?" and "my life is a mess" or you can get up, take a deep breath, affirm that you can overcome whatever it is that is bothering you, take some physical action — and change your mind. Sometimes it really is that simple.

CHAPTER 9 — COMMITMENT
AND SELF-DISCIPLINE

Very few worthwhile things in this life come about quickly or in a short period of time. It takes a certain amount of effort on your part and the discipline and commitment to keep at it. Sometimes it may seem that a change in another person is very sudden, but in all likelihood it has been brewing for a long time and the person has either been working on the change consciously or subconsciously. When there seems to be an about-turn in someone's attitude, behavior or the results that he or she is getting, it is usually still a result of some level of commitment and self-discipline that that person has employed to help them make a change.

If you want to change your mind and really start turning your world around, you need to work at it consistently, every day. Positive thinking is a habit, just as negative thinking is a habit that you may have developed. The way you think today is not the way you have always thought and you were not born thinking in a particular way. Your upbringing and experiences have shaped your thinking and *you* have personally shaped your thinking. You might say that you are a negative thinker because of other people, such as your parents. This may be partly true and they may have had quite a bit to do with your negative thinking up to a point, but you are ultimately the person who is responsible for your own life. Once you reach a certain age where you begin thinking for yourself and questioning the ideas and motives of others, this is the same time when the responsibility shifts from external "others" to you alone.

There is simply no point in blaming others. Blame creates hate, resentfulness, and feelings of guilt. These emotions are anathema to the person who truly wants to become a positive thinker and they are apparently linked to many psychosomatic illnesses that you simply cannot afford to have.

You *can* change; you can become a better person, a happier person and change your life towards any direction you want.

What it takes is:

1. Acknowledging that your thinking is wrong or being able to recognise your negative automatic thoughts — as I have detailed in a previous chapter.

2. Determining that you will no longer be ruled by these thoughts.

3. Creating in yourself a *burning desire* to change.

4. *Consistently and courageously* applying positive thinking and thought conditioning to your life. Having the discipline to make it happen even when the going gets tough.

Commitment to any given activity is a must for the successful person. You should give yourself 100 percent towards any particular task or activity you are engaged in. Whether it's work, a hobby, or being with friends. You must concentrate your mind and body on one activity at a time.

Many times in the past I remember going to a tae kwon do class with many things weighing heavily on my mind. I have found that if I start to think about anything else (e.g., my studies, my life, my job) I become distracted and sense a tension inside which seems to be saying to me: "Why are you here when you know you've got so much work to do?" This kind of thinking can paralyze your effort to relax, work out, or do whatever else you might be trying to do. Most often it's when you are trying to relax or do something you enjoy.

What I have done in these situations is take control of my thoughts and effectively say this right back to that little voice inside:

"Now look here. I have come to train for the next hour and a half. Everything else in my life can wait until I get home or until I need to deal with that specific area. I will not have my relaxation/physical fitness time destroyed by such negative and anxious thinking."

I then usually proceed to give my best to the training session, my mind quiets down, and I really enjoy my hour and a half away from the rest of my life.

I find the following quote quite useful in this regard:

"One step enough for me."

We must realize that everything has a time and a place. You should never try and do more than one thing at a time. This does not mean that you can't have a whole bunch of projects on the go at the same time. What it means is that if you are dealing with project number 1, you must concentrate completely on that project. You can move to number 2 later, and then you concentrate completely on number 2.

It wastes your time and energy and it can also leave you feeling torn if you are busy with project one and you are trying to think about how you are going to handle project two at the same time. It doesn't work, it's not efficient, so don't do it.

If you deal with each part of your life in its allotted time, giving yourself fully to that part while you are engaged in it, you will find that you can start to enjoy each part more and more. You start to lose that sense of tension that you create by being in one place and thinking about being in another. This is especially important when it comes to being with friends and family. It is so important to use that time wisely and not waste it by not being with them 100 percent. People can often sense when we are not completely there and when we are distracted by something else. Our lack of "mindfulness'" can lead to feelings of frustration and hurt, *especially if a loved one is trying to tell us something and we are not really listening*. Work must never dominate your life so much so that it intrudes on your moments alone with friends or family. Like I said, it wastes your time, and more importantly it takes away from the richness of the other activity you are engaged in.

To explain further the value of commitment and self-discipline, let me again use an example from the seven years experience I have in tae kwon do. You can learn so much about human behavior and personality when you take part in a tae kwon do class over a period of years, or any martial art for that matter. When I first began doing tae kwon do, I was not the fastest or the best athlete in the world — far from it! I often struggled to run up the hills when we did our fitness training and I had to keep working really hard on my kicks to try and get them right. I would often get very frustrated when a kick we had been learning for a few years wasn't working out for me. There were others in the class, however, who seemed to be able to do the hardest kicks with the greatest of ease and with the greatest confidence. There were a few guys in the class who had started at roughly the same time as I did. They had a definite talent for tae kwon do and I suppose for sports in general. They kicked really well, were super-fit and often became the "favourites" of the tae kwon do instructor. What I noticed, however, as the years went by, was that no matter how fast they came out kicking (if you will excuse the expression) and no matter how brilliant they were, after a certain amount of time they would leave. It didn't matter that they may have been the most talented people, with the most potential to become world champions at tae kwon do; if they didn't have what it took mentally to stick it out and to have the discipline to see it through, then all the talent in the world was for nothing.

I, on the other hand, who began with maybe a little less talent and athletic prowess, began to improve and get better over the years. Eventually my kicks started becoming really accurate and powerful. My confidence improved as I got better and one day, after having seen how my skills compared to other clubs and belts, I realised how far I had come and that the discipline and commitment that I put into tae kwon do had paid off. I gained so many other benefits from doing tae kwon do (such as the levels of physical fitness I achieved and the confidence) but the one thing that it really taught me was the value of being disciplined and committed to doing something and seeing it through. Now, please bear in mind that I am not saying that you must remain committed to something even when you feel it no longer serves you or when it has started to become a real drain on you. You will need to walk that line carefully and continuously test the waters to see whether what you are doing is benefiting you and whether you are achieving your goals in life. There came a time for me when I decided to leave tae kwon do when I felt it no longer — at that moment — served me. I may well return to it someday, but I made the decision to leave after doing it for seven years. My instructor had returned to France and I felt that the class was no longer teaching me and helping me grow. The difference was that I stuck it out and really enjoyed the benefits I gained from tae kwon do even though there were so many times I wanted to quit.

I remember my very first day, our instructor made us do frog jumps across the dojo for ten minutes and we ran around doing sit-ups, push-ups, and all kinds of other hectic exercises. I remember running outside and being sick in the parking lot. I hadn't done any real hard exercise for a long time, if ever. My friend who introduced me to the class came out and asked me if I was okay. I told him that if I had wanted to join the army I would have signed up for the army! I was pretty sure in my mind that I wasn't coming back to the class. I did return for the next class, however, because I really wanted to learn tae kwon do and because I wanted to finally make a commitment to something and stick with it. I had tried judo when I was very young and kung fu when I was in my teens and this time I wanted to give it my best shot. I kept returning for the next seven years and made it to black belt, which I saw as a major achievement considering how difficult the class was and how hard the instructor could be at times.

As another example, I know a young man who is extremely talented when it comes to music. He was born with a "musical ear." By age 11, he was playing Queen's "Bohemian Rhapsody" on the piano just from listening to it and then learning it by trial and error on the piano. Later in life he taught himself the guitar and then the electric guitar. There was a time I didn't see him for a period of a year or so because he was overseas and when he came back he had learned to play the electric guitar on his own and he was playing the likes of Gary Moore and Santana. He played them almost to a tee! But this young man has never learned the discipline to stick to something and he is always getting himself into some form of trouble or another. There is no doubt in my mind that he has the potential to reach rock star status if he even had a little discipline to see it through and to make it happen for himself. It really is such a pity to see talent go to waste. I believe that we all have innate potential and the seeds of greatness in us, but it is the discipline and commitment to water those seeds and to develop those talents that is needed before any measure of success will come about. I don't think you will often find people who have made it to the top in any field who have not spent a lot of time grooming and preparing themselves to be there. They probably spent hours and hours, days, months and even years preparing themselves and taking steps along the way before they finally "made it."

There is no doubt that life requires us to put in the time to reap the rewards. We often have to keep going when we feel that there is nothing left in us to move us forward. As a line from Edgar A. Guest's poem goes: "It's when you're hardest hit that you mustn't quit."

At times like these, when you are faced with a difficult path in your journey or when you come up against an obstacle that seems like it cannot be overcome, you may find yourself thinking that you should quit. When you come to that moment you can often see how your life is at a crossroads and that one decision will take you one way and the other decision another way. Although I must admit that most people probably wouldn't take the time to think about which way their decisions are going to take them in life. It can be a very emotional time when you are on that brink and you feel like its just so much easier to let it go and to give up. But don't do it, not unless you are very sure that this is no longer what you want for yourself. A useful thing to remember and to say to yourself when you are in this kind of situation is to say that it is very easy to quit and give up. Remind yourself that you always have the choice to quit and give up but it takes someone with that little bit of something in them to carry on going when the going gets tough and that you are one of those people. The option to quit is there, your escape button will always be there but you can make the decision to not use it just yet (keep it like an ace up your sleeve) and stick it out and stay committed. Again this is assuming that the thing you want to stay committed to is good for you and for your development and growth.

You will always look back on your ability to stick with something and realize that you have a lot of strength and staying power within you. The best thing is that it's a transferable skill. It does not only apply to the activity or goal you are working on at the moment. Once you learn to flex your discipline and commitment "muscles," you can learn to transfer those skills to other areas of your life. I found that my discipline in tae kwon do gave me extra discipline when it came to completing my honours and master's degrees. If you decide that you want to begin an exercise regime, there is no doubt that you will need to develop your discipline "muscles" as well as your actual muscles. If you want to learn how to play the guitar or how to play golf, you will need that discipline and commitment to carry on.

Commitment and discipline are directly related to the level of motivation that you can create for yourself to get yourself moving. Motivation and discipline are two sides of the same coin. It's an intricate relationship that can be useful to understand. The really important thing to take note of is the effect that discipline has on motivation. It will be the levels of discipline that you can create in your life that will allow you to lift your levels of motivation, and not usually the other way around. As an example, I am sure that very few of you have not experienced the lack of motivation to go and do a physical activity. Whether that activity is going to the gym, going for a jog, going for a swim, taking the dog for a walk, going for a walk, or even taking out the trash. When we feel low with motivation to do something, it is our level of discipline that will get us to get up and get going. It's also an intricate play going on in your mind about the pros and cons of actually getting up and doing it. Your mind starts to play mental football, knocking around the ball and trying to find enough reason or motivation to make it happen. When you have spent enough time developing the discipline and have learned to put this mental game on the side and focus on why you *want* to do your activity and how you will feel afterwards rather than the reasons you don't want to do it, you will find it becoming easier and easier to just get up and go because that is what you are doing. You create a routine in your life (not a boring one but a disciplined one) that helps you to get going without too much mental ping pong.

One of the benefits of developing your skills at being disciplined and committed is increasing your ability to achieve your goals and desires. When you know that you have what it takes to make it happen in your life and when you start to see yourself as a disciplined person and thus a successful person, you will really begin to change your mind and get your life moving in the right direction.

CHAPTER 10 — AFFIRMATIONS

Much has been written about the use of affirmations, so this chapter is not going to be any in-depth discussion about them. It will, however, explain their use in relation to how they can help you change your mind by thought replacement. When you learn how to stop negative thoughts in their tracks, your mind will want to fill the vacuum or gap with something else and this is where you would employ some really effective affirmations.

Affirmations work firstly on your conscious mind and help to immediately change and alter how you feel. Our aim, however, is to use really effective affirmations that deal with your beliefs so that we can, over a period of time, get the affirmations to sink below the level of conscious awareness into the deeper levels of your psyche: we want to get to your subconscious mind. Some of the most useful affirmations that I have come across as well as some that I have created will be included below. Feel free to use my affirmations or, once you get the hang of it, create your own! What you need to keep in mind about creating affirmations is that you need to keep them focused on the here and now, keep them stated in the positive and make them close to reality but a little bit better. Let me explain what I mean. If you have an affirmation that is put in the negative, for example: "I will not smoke another cigarette ever again," that affirmation uses the words "smoke," "cigarette," and "not." Your subconscious and conscious minds will hear the words and picture the smoke and cigarette and probably make you want to smoke even more. However, if you had created an affirmation such as: "I fill my lungs with healthy, clean air and I am enjoying breathing easily, every day. I can walk and run easily and effortlessly." Now that's an effective affirmation! You are telling your conscious and subconscious how much pleasure you are getting out of living healthily, breathing in fresh air and when you try to think about smoking, your mind will reel against it because you have created a stronger picture in your mind of why breathing in clean air is more important to you.

Below I have included for you some affirmations, grouped in themes that you may find useful. The best time to use them is either in meditation or when your mind feels like it is full of negativity. Try and find out what you are thinking (i.e., what your negative automatic thoughts are about), then try to clear your mind before you start doing these affirmations. When you say them, try to say them out loud while you focus on what they mean to you. If you just read them off the page, I'm afraid I don't think they will do you much good. You must make them your own by thinking about what they mean and imagining vividly in your mind what the affirmation is referring to. The more often you can use these affirmations, the more likely they are to sink deeper into your subconscious mind and begin to change your long held beliefs which may have been stopping you from having or getting what you want in your life. I am not saying that affirmations are guaranteed to change your life straight away or that they are the secret key to everything, what I am saying is that they are very helpful in breaking a negative thought pattern. They will help your mind realise that there are other more rational and positive ways to think about each situation you are having difficulty with.

The important thing to remember when you do affirmations is that you can't do them half-heartedly; you must say them with passion. If there are people around you and you don't want to be embarrassed shouting out in front of them, then say it loudly in your head with energy and passion. Say it like you mean it. When you say the words, try to concentrate on what it is you are saying and picture something in your mind that matches with what you are saying.

For example, if you have the flu and you decide you want to use a healing affirmation, then you might say, "Every day in every way I am feeling better and better," and while you are saying this, imagine yourself feeling better. Picture what you would be doing and the look on your face as you are now feeling better. By saying an affirmation with passion and picturing what you are saying in your mind, you will be quite surprised at how quickly things will change for you or get better. Your mind will always try to complete a mental picture you make and to find ways to bring that picture into physical reality so you can choose what you want your mind to focus on.

The following pages are some examples you can use for different situations in your life. But why not try to make up some of your own? Just remember to keep them in the present, positive, and filled with what you want, not what you don't want.

For when you feel that there is not enough to go around or when you feel you are lacking in something:

For Abundance:
I have unlimited access to the abundance of the universe.
I am open to receiving all that God and the universe have to offer me.
Money flows to me in avalanches of abundance.
I release money with joy and it returns to me a thousand fold.
I see abundance all around me; I am a part of that abundance.
There is plenty for everyone including me.
I deserve the best.
I now move into the winner's circle.

For Peace and Success:
I created this affirmation, which I think has a very powerful combination of many different issues that we all deal with, namely: fear of not having enough, anxiety about the future, worrying whether we will ever find our true calling and feeling tense and worried.

This affirmation is the antidote to all those, all rolled up in one, enjoy it! I call it:

"My affirmation for Peace and Success"

"I am confident that I am achieving my goals each and every day. Every little action I take is leading me towards my dreams and goals. I take each day calmly, smoothly and in God's unhurried tempo. I enjoy each day that God has given me on this earth to the fullest. I am happy, joyful and peaceful both internally and externally. I attract my highest path through living each day with a high resonance. I trust in God and his universe and I believe that I will be led to my highest path and I will achieve success just as I have imagined it and so much more!"

(Feel free to copy this affirmation and paste it on a wall where you can see it every morning and every night).

To reduce anxiety and worry:

I trust that everything is happening exactly as it should.
God is with me, God is guiding me, God is helping me.
Everything happens for a reason and a purpose and it serves my highest good.
I let go and I trust that this will work out for the best.
If I have faith, anything is possible for me.
I always take the right turn in the road.

To increase health:

The healing powers of God are within me.
My body has universal intelligence and knows how to heal itself.
The same magical powers that created my body are still within me and able to heal me.
I love every part of my body.
Every day in every way I feel better and better.
I look after my body every day through healthy eating, exercise, and lots of water.

I am sure you will find these useful. What you might want to try is to take one that you like from each category and write them down on little cards. Keep these cards with you in your pocket, purse, or wallet and refer to them often. Once you know them by heart, you can throw the card away. Go for it! If you want more affirmations or help in making your own, feel free to drop me an email at david@foxpsychology.com.au

CHAPTER 11 — GETTING HELP FROM A HIGHER SOURCE

A psychology counselling book would most likely avoid any discussion surrounding God or any higher source of help for us when we are in our greatest hour of need. The fact is that very few people would say that they have not at one time or another asked for help or guidance from whatever higher power or source they believe in. Sometimes it can be very difficult to deal with some of the issues we have to deal with as human beings and often it can all seem too much to cope with. Without our belief in a higher power or source of inspiration and a belief that there is a reason for everything that happens in our lives, life can seem to be very difficult, unfair, and meaningless.

I know that I for one have had many moving times in my life where I have felt that I was at my lowest point and where I could not see a way forward no matter how hard I tried. When I was told, after having arrived in London with my wife, that I would need to undergo an operation called an osteotomy or risk losing all my teeth before I turned forty, I was quite shocked, as you might imagine! It involves the maxillo-facial surgeon slicing through the skull and moving the top part of the jaw forward. I needed to have this done because my teeth were touching against each other dead-on instead of the upper teeth coming down over the bottom teeth. I had had orthodontics twice in my life and I had been struggling with a painful condition called TMJ (temporomandibular joint), which is a disorder of the muscles and bones of the jaw. This can lead to a number of complications, including the jaw clicking and popping, ringing in the ears (also known as tinnitus) and painful cheek and jaw muscles. I was suffering from all of these and so had begun my second round of orthodontics at the age of 27, one month after I got married and just a few short months before my wife and I emigrated to London. I never knew before we left that I would need the operation. I only found out once I went to see my new orthodontists in London. They advised me that the orthodontics would not do much good if I did not have the operation. I remember leaving their office in Stanmore, new to London and still without a job, having to now pay for orthodontics, which would already start costing us about one hundred pounds a month and now I was being told I needed a major operation. Strangely enough, at that point, I didn't react too badly and put into practice some of what I have learned about handling some of the curve balls that life throws at us. I told myself that: "What must be, must be, and we will handle it and make a plan." When I got back home, I told Michelle what had happened and she too at that point just said that we would have to see what we could do about it.

Many months later, the pain and the agony of my ears ringing and the tense and stiff muscles in my jaw and face were becoming too much for me to bear. I decided that I needed to fly back to South Africa and have the operation done by a maxillo-facial surgeon there for two reasons: 1.We could not afford to pay for it in pounds and 2. Even if it could be covered under National Health, I might be 99 before my appointment to see the surgeon ever came around and I just wasn't prepared to wait that long!

So, we called up the maxillo-facial surgeon and got a quote for the operation. Although it was a lot of money (even in pounds!), we thought that with a little bit of savings we could afford to do it with the conversion from pounds to rands, which was quite favourable at 10 rand to the pound at that stage. So the appointment was booked for April 1, 2004. I booked my flight and when the time came, I had to quit my job, as I was going to need a lot more time to recover than I could reasonably expect in leave — and I really hated my job anyway! So although we really had to take the bitter pill of losing some of the savings we had worked for in London, we thought it was an amount we could handle and still come back to London to save for our eventual emigration to Sydney.

I arrived in South Africa before my wife did. She was to join me two weeks later. I went about making enquiries about the operation and then asked the maxillo-facial surgeon's secretary to fax me a quote for the operation. I remember it very clearly, I was at my friend's house. His mother was also there. The fax came through and as I tore it off and scanned my eyes down to the bottom line I nearly had a heart attack. I think I started saying: "Oh my God, Oh my God." If you have ever seen a movie where someone is about to faint from shock and you don't think its possible, well neither did I until that moment. I felt like my whole life was crashing in on me and flashing before my eyes. You see, I was really counting on this operation to heal me and to help get me out of the immense discomfort and pain I had been experiencing for the past few years. I was pinning all my hopes on this finally being the answer and when I saw that bill it was almost three times more expensive than originally quoted. Now I don't know why this happened or how this happened. I don't know if the surgeon had originally thought he was only quoting one part of the operation which was maybe his own fee alone and not hospital fees, additional help in the theater fees and the actual titanium pins that needed to be used to hold my jaw together afterwards. For whatever reasons, the quote was so high that at that point I thought there was no way. I started to waver and it was my friend's mom –– bless her —who started shouting at me: "Stop it! Stop it" in her thick Israeli accent. She basically used what Tony Robbins would call a pattern interrupt on me and shocked me back out of my shock!

When my mind started teeming with having to tell my wife what the quote was while she was still in London, I started to feel sick. Anyway, to finally get to the point of this story, which I am sure you are wondering about....I went home to my parents' house and went out into the back yard. I decided that if ever there was a time to practice some of the stuff I had learned it was now. Now, the thing was, we did have the money in pounds to be able to pay for the operation, but it would totally wipe us out and leave us with nothing. No new life to start in Sydney and nothing to show for our efforts in London. I needed some inspiration and guidance because I really felt as if I wasn't going to make it through this one. So I sat down in the garden and began to get quiet. I stopped all thoughts in my mind and I asked God to help me with this. I told him that this decision was too big for me and I just didn't know what to do. It didn't take long before a very gentle thought entered my mind. It didn't seem like a thought that would have come from me at that point in time. The thought that popped into my head was:

"If money was no object for you and you could afford to have this operation, would you have it?" My answer was obviously yes. The next thought was: "Then what is the problem? Because you can afford to have it." From that point on, I realised once again that we cannot know what the greater plan is for our lives. I knew that had we stayed in South Africa and not gone to London, there was no physical way I could ever have afforded to have the operation without going into massive debt and that maybe that was one of the reasons I had felt such a strong pull to go to London.

Later on, once my wife had arrived, we went to see the surgeon and explained our situation. He did his best to reduce the bill and we ended up paying quite a bit less than the original quote. I had the operation. I don't think I will go into the details of the actual operation or how scared I was before it and the nightmare of a recovery I had afterwards, but let me just impress upon you how we truly do have a deeper wisdom inside us. The actual operation itself was a success in terms of my jaw being placed correctly and the popping and clicking stopped, as did the tinnitus.

Whether you believe in God or not, there are times in all of our lives where we feel the touch of something miraculous, something that cannot just be explained away as mere coincidence. If you think about it, how many people in the world do you think are religious or spiritual or believe in a higher power that is there for us and is guiding us? I don't have a clue but I am willing to bet it's the vast majority of the world's population. Within that population are some of the most brilliant, scientific and practical people on earth and they also believe in the support of a higher power. I believe it was Socrates who said after his life's journey, "if logic tells you that life is a meaningless set of coincidences, don't give up on life, give up on logic."

Let me just say now that I am not a very religious person but I do often feel and I like to believe that there truly is a higher power. I have seen so many examples of miraculous events occur in my own life and I bet you have too. I also bet you that there were times in your life where you felt like things would never get better or where you felt like your problems were intractable and then something happened to help you resolve them. When you look back on your life and think about all the "chance" encounters, all the people you have met and who may have loved you or helped you through I think you will start to agree with me that there is a source of help we can turn to in our deepest and darkest hours of need. Even when our need is not so great, I believe that God or whatever/whoever you believe in is there for you and me and when you ask, you will be answered, just take some time to get quiet inside so you don't miss the answer.

CHAPTER 12 — BRINGING IT ALL TOGETHER... LIFE'S TETRAHEDRON©

A tetrahedron is one of the most stable forms in nature and science. The pyramids in Egypt that have stood for thousands of years have managed to stay that way partly due to that fact that they are shaped as tetrahedrons. I thought that this would be very apt to describe to you how the four major areas of our lives all need focus and that once you are working on all of these, you will start to see some major positive changes happening in your life.

Life's Tetrahedron©

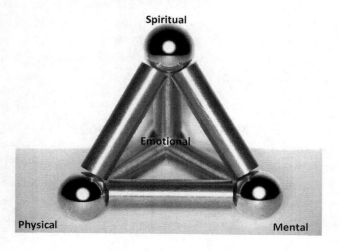

111

If you focus on one, two, or three of the triangles, you might get a certain amount of change, but it is quite likely that it would only do so much in helping you to really make significant changes. If you were to focus on all four triangles of the tetrahedron, you would get massive and long-lasting change. The four triangles are inextricably linked to each other in life. You decide that you want to make a change in your life, let's say you want to lose weight. So, you start an exercise regime and you are pretty fired up about it. Here you are focusing on the physical triangle only. You start working out every second or third day and you notice some results in your body. After a few weeks of doing this, you are finding that you haven't lost that much weight and you begin to worry whether there is something wrong with you. What you haven't done in this case is work on your thoughts around food and exercise. It will be quite hard to keep up your gruelling exercise or diet if you haven't developed the ability to talk to yourself in a positive and encouraging way. You might start being hard on yourself, especially if you miss a day of exercise or eat an extra piece of cake and then your inner critical voice just comes down on you. You then move into the emotional triangle and all hell breaks loose. You get upset, frustrated and angry and start to think that you want to give up your exercise regime and forget about the diet. This probably makes you feel even worse and so the cycle continues. So you can see, if you want to make changes, lasting changes that is, you will want to think about each part of the tetrahedron and write down what you can do in that triangle to support the change you want to make in your life.

Each triangle has been represented in some form throughout this book. I have discussed the value of physical exercise, the spiritual side of life, the cognitive approach to changing your mind, and what to do about emotions.

I have consistently spoken about the connection between the physical and emotional triangles. Where you work on one, you will also be helping the other. For example, when you exercise, you allow your mind time to rest and rejuvenate and sometimes you need to set up new beliefs about exercise to help you get motivated to go out and do it. I know that there are people, especially women, who don't like the thought of going jogging or doing any exercise that requires becoming sweaty. But if they want to achieve real results with any exercise regime they will need to sweat a little. By changing what they associate with the concept of sweating, they should be able to get themselves to do it. For example, if they decide to create a new belief about sweating that associates it with becoming thinner or healthier or that every time they feel themselves sweating from exercise they are getting closer to fitting into that dress they want to wear, they have created a powerful positive association. This will help drive them to work out and not mind so much about the sweating part!

While I referred to the spiritual side of life earlier in the book and mentioned that everyone at one time or another has called upon a higher power for strength or help, the spiritual triangle can also be seen in a different light and that is the light of meaning and purpose in life. If you are running endlessly on the treadmill of life (literally and figuratively!), and you are running from one activity or relationship to another, you may feel that there is something missing. Many people who achieve great "success" by becoming very famous or rich arrive at their goals and find that it all feels quite empty and meaningless. There have been too many rock stars that have had everything that you and I have dreamed of, everything you can possibly imagine at their fingertips, and who still felt that life was empty, meaningless, and ended up quitting life. How sad! How tragic that these people who managed to use so much of their physical and cognitive skills in life to achieve great success didn't understand that they needed to create meaning for themselves and to understand that some of the happiest people in the world are often those who don't actually have much. They are often people who have decided that life is truly worth living in the moment and that life can be fun and joyful every day — just because they want it to be. I am sure you have come across people like this in your life, people who seem to exude a joy and peace in life regardless of what is happening to them. It has always been one of my goals to become like those people. To live purely in the moment and realize that the moment is all you really have. Being alive is such a gift and the meaning that you attach to it is entirely up to you. Remember that no matter what you have been before or what your upbringing was, you can decide to change your mind today and become whoever you want to be! If you are feeling like you are drifting aimlessly through life and that you are demotivated and frustrated, the best cure for that is to re-frame the way you see your life and the meaning that you attach to it. Read *Man's Search for Meaning* by Victor Frankl if you want a quick kick in the pants. It will show you that you don't have it so bad and you always have the choice to create a reason for living in life. I love the quote I once read somewhere that says: "How do you know if you still have a purpose on earth? If you are still alive, you do."

CHAPTER 13 — DEALING WITH CHANGE AND LETTING GO — EVEN WHEN YOU AREN'T SURE OF THE OUTCOME

Change can be really scary, whether it is change for the better or change that seems like it's for the worse. The hardest part of making a change, or dealing with a change that has happened in our lives, is learning to deal with the uncertainty of the outcome. We all tend to worry about how things are going to turn out and no matter how many times they actually do turn out well, we keep going through the same fears every time change is upon us. We need to learn to trust the process of life. We need to learn that when we are flying in the air between the two bars of the trapeze, it's going to feel uncomfortable and we are going to feel like it's all gone wrong. However, it's just the "in-between" space and we will soon grab hold of that bar and carry on — often being better off than when we started.

In this chapter you will be given some techniques for how to deal with change in your life and examples from some of my own most trying moments will be given to emphasize how change usually leads to bigger and better things, and yes, that it usually is for our greatest good.

Sometimes all our planning and goal setting can force us into seeing our lives in only a few dimensions instead of all the wonderful colorful dimensions that life can be made up of. We need to understand that it's okay to make plans and to set really high goals for ourselves, but only under one condition. That condition is what will keep us sane and happy and help us to avoid becoming disturbed, stressed or burned out because we feel sometimes that we are not achieving as much as we should be and we are not where we wanted to be by now.

The most important thing that you may need to learn to do is to create your goals and then forget you ever made them and live your life every day in appreciation and gratitude for where you are right now, not for where you want to be. I have had to learn this trick the hard way. I am very forward thinking by nature and I like to have a plan and an outcome for everything. I like to see or know where things are going. I don't know if you have come across a personality profile called the MBTI (Myers Briggs Type Indicator)? It's a really great tool for shedding some light on the differences between people and it is based on the theory and research of Carl Jung. It breaks people down into 16 major groupings made up of four letter codes. My four letter code used to be ENTJ — E = extrovert (although I'm more borderline between extrovert and introvert); N = intuition; T = thinking; and J = judging. Now the letter that is of most interest here is the J. Judges like to have things ordered and understandable. The opposite of a Judge is a Perceiver. The perceiver (my ex-wife for example) can basically pack her bags and get on a plane for Europe and not know where she is going to stay, how she will get anywhere and what she will do when she gets to her destination. Perceivers love leaving everything to the last minute and letting things take care of themselves. This is a *huge* problem for the Judge. People with this characteristic in their personality like to make lists, they like to know precisely what the plan is and pretty much try and predict what will happen with some measure of certainty. No one characteristic is better than the other and the most important thing to do is to learn from the other profile and incorporate as much as you can so as to balance yourself and not be too extreme on any one characteristic. If you are interested, there are many excellent books on type that may be found in libraries or on the internet.

As you can see, the reason I say I have had to learn this lesson the hard way is that one can never predict exactly what is going to happen in any situation. We cannot know with certainty what will happen tomorrow, never mind next year, or even ten years from now. So, it is important to set your goals and imagine them vividly *but* it is just as important to learn to forget you ever set them and to allow yourself to enjoy your life right now without stressing about whether you are achieving your goals each day. If you do, your life may become very rigid and you may start living your life by rules and regulations that you formed many years ago and haven't taken the time to revise. Do not ever let your goals control your life; *you* must control your goals. It's fine to look at your goals once every six months or even a year and set new ones, but don't be so focused on them that you take away your enjoyment of everything that is going on around you right now. Your reality right now is the manifestation of your previous goals and you are living that reality right now. Don't lose your appreciation for what you have already achieved by merely continuing to look forward. STOP. Right now I want you to acknowledge that everything around you that you see is a result of a decision you made or a goal you set previously. It may even be a subconscious goal or wish. Appreciate your ability to create. Appreciate the control you have and at the same time appreciate that there are things you could not foresee that happened and often turned out to be the best for you. It's all about balance isn't it? We can set our goals, visualise what we want and strive to achieve our goals, pushing harder and harder and sometimes getting really anxious when we think or feel that our goals might not be achieved but then we need to learn to balance that with the understanding and the ability to let go and let the universe take its course. Don't hold so tightly to one set of goals that you miss out on the ability to enjoy what you have created right now in front of your eyes. The more you can focus on enjoying each minute of your life and letting go, the easier your life will flow and the easier it will be in the end to achieve the larger goals of your life. When you can work towards your goals without obsessively focusing on them but by just enjoying your life — you will begin to learn that delicate balance that brings about joy and peace in your life instead of stress, pushing, anxiety, and worry.

I would like to focus now a little deeper on this process of when to push and when to let go and I am going to include some spiritual principles.

Let me say again that the hardest thing to do when you are faced with an uncertain outcome and when the stakes are high is to know when to push forward and when to stop and watch the effects of your effort take hold and manifest. The reason it is so hard can be understood again by understanding that there is a time lag or delay between an action and a response. I do believe that when we have reached the end of our rope and feel as if we have tried everything in the book to make something happen and it's still not happening, that we need to realize something. That something is that in the spiritual world, things don't happen according to our worldly conception of how time works and how reactions to events work. We usually believe that there is a direct and visible relationship between action and outcome. Yehuda Berg, in his excellent book *The Power of Kaballah,* explains this issue of a time lag or delay between our actions and the outcome. You may feel like you have poured all your heart and soul into something and there appears to be no immediate reward or positive outcome. You may feel, as I have on so many occasions, that you have done everything you were supposed to. In other words, you took action, you prayed, you stayed positive and said your affirmations, you visualised and meditated and *still* it hasn't "worked." You need to take a step back from all your activity, take a deep breath and keep still. Remember to occupy yourself with some other meaningful pursuit and let go of the outcome. Truly, when you have done all you feel is necessary you may need to take a breather and wait for some fresh inspiration, but if you keep pushing and pushing, harder and harder, all you are going to do is wear yourself down and lose your motivation. I know exactly what this is like. Let me give you an example, one I feel you will probably relate to or know someone who it would relate to.

When I first left South Africa and went to live in London, my ex-wife and I went there without any jobs lined up. We had enough money to last a few months. We also didn't have a place to stay and knew that we would only be staying with some friends for a week or two. At that stage of our lives we had decided to go first to London before emigrating to Sydney, Australia, and settling down. We went over with a very large dose of optimism and trust that everything would work out for us. However, what we didn't count on was the job market in London being very depressed and still feeling the effects of September 11, 2001. All we had heard from people was how easy it was to get a job in London. So when it started taking us longer and longer to find jobs, we started to feel a little panicky. We were quickly eating into our funds and didn't know what was going to happen. We couldn't very well go back to South Africa because we had emigrated! We had packed up our things, sold our cars, left both our jobs and had nothing really to go back to besides our friends and families. This was a very trying time for both of us, but after a few more weeks we both found work. Although it wasn't the ideal work, it paid the bills and we were able to live in London for the next 18 months or so before we decided it was time to come and settle down in Sydney.

When I first arrived in Sydney, it only took me two months to find a job. Michelle then found a two-day-a-week job. I didn't like my first job, and it was far from home so I looked for and found another one at a large insurance company in a role I had not really done before, but which I thought would be great for my career growth. I took a drop in salary to take on this role and although this didn't please us, we felt the long-term benefits would outweigh the decrease in salary. What happened then was like my worst nightmare come to life. Before leaving my last job, we found out that Michelle was pregnant with our first child. So now we had just emigrated to a new country and we were also about to become parents for the first time. We were both very excited about the prospect of having a baby and were looking forward to enjoying the pregnancy.

However, at work things started to go horribly wrong for me. The lady that had interviewed me who had seemed very nice and caring turned out to be a bully and control freak. After my second week, she started telling me that she "was very concerned" and that the work I was doing wasn't good enough. Without giving me clear guidance on what to do, she gave me some work on changing the performance management documents and when what I gave her wasn't what she had in mind she went away and did it herself over the weekend, totally ignoring the work I had done. Going to work became a nightmare and I dreaded getting up in the morning. I started to regret leaving my last job, where at least I had started to get into it and was building good relationships with the managers. I felt as if my whole world was falling apart and started to get very anxious and depressed. At this point I realised that I needed to do something quick. Thinking about everything I had learned in my life up to that point and following the lessons I believed I had learned in London about staying in a job too long that was not right for me, I decided I would rather quit the job than go through that ever again. Without another job to go to and knowing that Michelle was now four months pregnant, I decided to take one of the biggest leaps of faith I had ever taken in my life. I did however do this with the added knowledge that the recruitment market for HR professionals seemed to be particularly buoyant at that time and feeling certain that I would secure another job within a month.

The reality, however, turned out to be quite different. At first there seemed to be a flurry of activity with agents all telling me the market was flush with jobs and that it wouldn't take me long at all. Then I went for interviews to agencies and companies, without any luck. I did everything I could think of to apply for jobs. I met nearly every agency in Sydney and walked the streets of the city every week going from one agent and interview to another, but still not finding a job. Every now and then a role would look promising and the interview would seem to go well, but something kept blocking me from getting the position. It wasn't my interviewing skills because I got very good feedback. It was often things like them wanting someone with more in-depth experience in redundancies or them saying that I needed more Australian experience. (I love that catch-22 by the way!).

Time passed by and two and a half months later I still didn't have a job. At this point I had thrown everything in the book at the problem. I had visualised, meditated, prayed to God, taken immense amounts of action and retained my faith, trust, and optimism, but the results didn't seem to be adding up. Michelle was now almost seven months pregnant and I didn't have a job. I did have something on the go with a large human resource consultancy that seemed very promising. I had been for two interviews, psychometric testing, and was quite keen on the role, but the main problem was that the salary was about $20,000 per year less than the other HR jobs I had been applying for. But I really liked the company and it was a place I felt I could finally move into external human resource consulting and utilize my experience and knowledge both as an organizational psychologist and as an HR professional. I felt like the universe was playing a cruel game with me. All the roles that promised a great salary, which I sorely needed with a new baby on the way, weren't coming my way and the one job I really wanted didn't seem to want to pay enough for us to get by on.

It was at this point that I just didn't know what to do or how this situation was going to resolve itself in a way that would lead me to having a job I loved and for us to do well enough financially with a new baby on the way.

Every day I would go onto the internet and apply for more HR roles and every day I would get rejection letters in my inbox like this one:

Dear David

Thank you for your interest in the HR position.

Due to the large response we have received for this advertisement, we have had to be very specific in our criteria for establishing a short list for first interviews. Unfortunately, we are unable to include you in interviews for this position at this stage. Should our first round of interviews not provide us with the appropriate candidate we will review your application and contact you accordingly.

Additionally, we will keep your resume on file and should another position become available which meets your experience, we will contact you.

In future, should another of our advertised positions interest you, please do not hesitate to contact us.

Thank you once again for your application and we wish you all the very best in your job search.

You can only look at so many of these before your heart starts to sink and you actually start to wonder what the hell is wrong with you. Why does everyone else seem to be doing so much better? Why is this happening to me even though I have practiced every spiritual principle known to man? Are the principles all wrong? Do they only work some of the time or for a privileged few? Have I not done enough of this or that? Should I push harder? Surely, if I sit back now and wait for an outcome I will land myself up the creek without a paddle? In other words, I will land up on the streets in a homeless shelter with my wife crying and my newborn baby in my arms! Okay, maybe I wasn't thinking to that level of extremes yet, but I was definitely starting to eye out the ads for waiters and sandwich hands. This was the greatest test of my faith and trust ever. This was the greatest test of my belief that everything happens for a reason and it serves our higher good. This was my greatest test of my belief that every negative and seemingly catastrophic event in our lives has the seed of an equivalent and greater good. I tried to find the balance between taking action and letting go. I knew that I couldn't just sit idly by as our money quickly disappeared out of our bank account and wait for God to save me. Whenever my Aunt Cheryse had work for me, which was packing canned pet food at a supermarket, I would do it just to bring in some money and keep me busy for a day.

On top of all of this, we were going to have to move out of our townhouse because we had found out that there was going to be building demolition and construction of the house next door to us and we just couldn't be around for that with a newborn baby and Michelle being an asthmatic. We couldn't, however, do anything until I had a job. I don't think that the saying "stuck between a rock and a hard place" quite begins to explain how I was feeling at that point. I had many sleepless nights, waking up at 2 or 3 in the morning and not being able to get back to sleep. This was the first time in my life this had ever happened to me because I could usually get a good night's sleep no matter what was happening in my life. Not this time.

Not knowing the outcome is the hardest part of dealing with change in life. Holding onto your faith and trust — even when the world and universe seem to be conspiring against you to prove that your faith is ineffectual — is hard! When people start turning on you and saying "I told you so..." you may also feel as if you have made a terrible mistake. You may panic and feel as if more action is required. This may be the case depending on your situation but bear this in mind: Sometimes God's plan in making us push against a huge boulder in our way is not so much about moving the rock but more about making us have stronger muscles. Think about that for a minute and see if anything now makes a little more sense to you. Let me explain how it made more sense to me in this situation I have described and the meaning I attached to the process even though I still couldn't see the outcome. What I started to focus on was:

1. Facing my fear of boredom and depression.
2. Time to heal and take a breather after two years of stress and emigration.
3. Improving our relationship — dealing with key issues.
4. Spending more time with family, niece and nephew.
5. Learning how to handle rejection — completely!
6. Moving closer to one of my biggest goals in life — writing this book, etc...

It was a short time later that I was offered a three-month contract with a large and vibrant telecommunications company in North Sydney. They hired me to help them with their end of year performance management process and some other project work. Straight away I loved the place and the people. It's a dynamic, young company with a great culture. They also offered me a great daily rate to work as a contractor. I still didn't have any security about what would happen after the end of the contract, especially seeing that coincided directly with the birth date of our first child. I think most people would find that very nerve-wracking. What I found was that by employing the techniques I have spoken about in this book so intensely over the previous period, I had all but removed the fear of what would come next. I realised there was no point trying to figure out what would happen. What chance meeting or what perfect next role would come up? The only thing to do was to trust and let go. I would continue to look for other opportunities and be active. Over the same time period I got my registration in NSW to practice as a psychologist and had business cards printed. Using the same techniques, I decided there was no point worrying about how I was going to get clients, I would just let life move me in the right direction and it would happen in its own right time.

One of the most useful techniques I have used to help me cope with worrying about the future is to remember how many different things I have worried about in the past that never happened. I highly recommend that the next time you find yourself worrying about whether something is going to work out you sit down with a pen and piece of paper and do the following:

1. Think back over your life of all the times you were faced with a situation that you worried about. What was it?
2. Why were you worrying? What did you think was going to happen?
3. Did it happen as you thought it would? What really happened in the end?
4. Write down at least five such situations and I am willing to bet you that by the time you get to the fourth one you will start to sigh a deep breath of relief when you realize how much wasted time you have spent worrying about the future.

Remember: "Worry is the interest you are paying on a debt you might not owe!"

You start to realize that things do work out in their own weird way and that most of the time something that happened to you that you couldn't understand at the time becomes much clearer later on in your life. You may not know why tomorrow or the next day, but I bet in a few months or a year's time you will. The trick is to realise this when you are going through it and then stop worrying. You then need to trust that what is happening now or what might happen in the future will help serve your highest good.

Here's another quick example. When I first completed my studies, I had to do a one-year internship in order to register as a psychologist in South Africa. Competition for internships was fierce as there were very few organizations that offered them. I couldn't understand why some of the people I studied for my master's with got these great internships at these big corporate companies while I only managed to get one initially at a charity. I felt very low at the time and felt that my internship would never be adequate or measure up. A year later, I could easily tell you why that happened. I left the charity after a few months and re-started my internship at a company called Cheque Guarantee Services. Just one month later, I got a call from one of the ladies I worked with at the charity who said she had a very nice girl for me to meet. The rest is history and that girl became my wife. Not only did I get a wife out of the thing I thought was so bad, I also ended up staying at CGS for three years and became their human resource manager, which opened lots of doors for me later on. That is one example I could give you out of a hundred and I am sure you have plenty of your own. The trick is to use your past constructively to help you feel peaceful, calm, and optimistic about your own future. You have all the resources inside you, all you need to do is look at them differently to understand how truly amazing and miraculous your life has been already and how absolutely fantastic it can be in the future. But you only create that future from today, from right now in this moment which is the only moment where you can choose to change your life from.

CHAPTER 14 — ENJOYING YOUR SUCCESSES

If one does not stop every now and then to look behind at what one has achieved, it becomes a difficult job to keep oneself motivated. The kind of people who find this the most difficult thing to do are those who have set very high standards for themselves and never permit themselves to relax and enjoy the successes they have already amassed. If one keeps running forward, collecting prizes, but not stopping every now and then to "take a bow," life may become very hard, grueling, and tiresome.

It is often helpful when one is feeling like the going is really rough to look back at what has been overcome before. Not only does this dispel the anxiety and fear about what has to be done in the future, but it also tends to keep one motivated to aim for bigger and better successes.

One should never downplay one's achievements in life, which is something that I know I have done on many occasions and it is something that I am still working on. I remember in my second year at university I was quite worried about the fact that I would have to take a subject called RDA, or research design and analysis, which included a course on statistics. I was never very good at math during school so the thought of having to do this course in order to major in psychology was disconcerting to say the least. Well, the course ran for six months and I can remember how hard I had to concentrate just to follow what the lecturer was saying and we were told that we needed at least 65 percent to major in psychology. We were also told that there was an optional but "highly recommended" follow-up course called RDA 2 that would run the final six months of the year. What happened was that I got 76 percent for the RDA course that earned me a certificate of first class. Not only that, but I did the follow-up course and got 75 percent for that one. But did I congratulate myself on this achievement? No way! Most of the people who were with me in the RDA 2 course had also done well, so what did I tell myself? I told myself that it wasn't such a great achievement because so many others had achieved it too! Whenever someone congratulated me I tried to play it down because I felt they shouldn't get the wrong idea about me. In other words, they shouldn't think I had achieved something that great because it wasn't really such an achievement.

Only later on did I learn that this is one of the most destructive things you can do to your motivation and your self-esteem. Let's look at how I could have and should have thought about my achievement.

I had aced a course that I had previously been really worried about.

There were considerably more people who failed that course than those who got above 75 percent. Instead of looking at the certificate of first class as nothing significant I should have seen it as valuable evidence that I could achieve anything I put my mind to.

Today when I look at the certificates that hang on my wall, they remind me that I have achieved a certain amount of success in my life. When I look at them, I try to think about what I actually had to go through to get those pieces of paper onto my wall. I go back through my mind and think of the struggles and the obstacles I had to overcome to succeed and I realise their actual value. It's often hard to see such hidden value unless one remembers in such a way.

Never downplay your success and never let anyone else do it to you either. They are *your* successes and you earned them, no matter what kind of success, no matter how big and especially how small they might be. Give yourself a pat on the back and say "Well done, you did it!" Then you can move on to bigger and better things and you can rest assured that you will be adding the building blocks of your success together instead of hiding them away from yourself and then wondering why your mountain of success seems no bigger now than when you began building it so long ago.

I guess another reason people don't seem to ever stop and congratulate themselves is because they may have their values all backwards. People who focus on external achievements such as wealth, property and fancy gadgets will always be able to want more and to need to have more in order to stop and feel good about themselves, that's if they stop at all! On the other hand, if you were to value yourself for every time you did something nice for someone else or when you showed love and caring to your family or friends, you would soon be over flowing with pride on your accomplishments. The problem is that most people don't see these things as accomplishments at all. They think it is just normal and a given. However, there are plenty of people in the world who would rather hurt others than be kind and open-hearted. They would rather destroy than create and fight rather than work in harmony. If you are a person who loves others and cares about them then you already have plenty to be proud about. You are a good person and we need all the good people we can get here on earth! Can you see how you can start to enjoy who you are and what you are right now before you take even one step more towards your other goals? I hope so, because it then makes your other goals a lot less demanding and stressful. You don't worry so much about whether you will reach them as much as what you are doing along the way each day and what the quality of your day to day life is like.

You can only appreciate your life right now. You cannot say, "I will wait until some future date to feel good about myself and my achievements." You should feel that way right now by making sure what you consider to be important in life is valuable not only to you but to others and that doesn't mean people only. You might have done something to help an animal in distress or planted a tree or helped clean up a park. Whatever it was that you did out of the goodness of your heart, including giving of money to charity must be remembered by you and appreciated. And yes, they are your successes as a human being and you should be very proud of them.

Remember also to share in the successes of other people and guard yourself from becoming overly jealous about what other people around you are achieving or have already achieved. It's not a race or competition and the only person you should ever compare yourself to is yourself. If you want to compete against yourself, that's fantastic. You know that every time you take yourself to the next level you can be proud of yourself. So change your life today by remembering that you are already a success in so many ways. Well done!

CHAPTER 15 — "THE PRICE OF LIBERTY IS ETERNAL VIGILANCE"

Above is a statement that I recently came across while walking near my home in Sydney. As soon as I saw this sign it struck me how this statement relates not only to the human freedoms of physical safety and security but also to the intellectual freedom and security of our own peace of mind.

I remember writing a long time ago that once you have achieved a certain level of peace with yourself and with your mind or when you have managed to lift yourself out of a depression or rid yourself of anxiety, the price you must pay from then on is eternal vigilance. What does vigilance mean in this context? Well, first let me explain what it might mean in the context of the Jewish people after the Holocaust. That statement would most aptly capture the spirit of why Israel was established as a state. It is because the Jewish people at that time, just after World War II, decided that the terrible atrocities that were committed upon them should never be allowed to happen ever again. The armed forces of Israel stand ready to do battle to ensure that never again can the people of Israel be persecuted. That, however, is the price of the freedom that they won by being granted a Jewish state by the United Nations. They have to maintain their vigilance and keep on the look out for danger.

If we were to apply this to you and your life, you might say that the example I have chosen above is extreme, but I am here to say to you: Is it not just as important to you that you stay out of your depression? That you continue to live a life free from anxiety and excessive worry? That you continue to find ways to create the life you want and that you deserve? Then, if you agree that these things are crucial, you will also agree that you too need to be vigilant when it comes to ensuring that what you have learned and hopefully practiced in this book is constantly used. You cannot learn the techniques, practice them for a few weeks or months and then — when you have achieved excellent results — get lazy and decide that you don't need to consciously work at it anymore. Beware. Even if you feel that things are totally under control and your emotions are all positive and peaceful, you need to keep looking out for negative automatic thoughts, faulty beliefs —which may still be lurking around — and self-defeating behavior patterns.

Remember, when you catch yourself falling into the negative thinking trap, or when you suddenly realize you haven't been doing any meditation for the past two weeks, this is not a time to chastise yourself. It is a time to congratulate yourself on remembering that you are not being vigilant and immediately reaffirm your commitment to taking the actions you need to take to ensure that your life continues on the path you have now chosen. Do not get down on yourself if at first you slip up and return to old ways or bad habits. This is to be expected and it is part of the whole process. In fact, this is a required part of the syllabus of making personal change a reality in your life. If you don't have any setbacks then I think your problems probably weren't as bad as you may have thought in the first place!

Everyone who struggles with a difficult issue will have setbacks and times when they feel that everything is not working. When you feel that all your hard work is not paying off, just remember that you cannot see a seed growing underground until it bursts through the earth. Just keep at it. Releasing yourself from an emotional and mental prison is not easy but you can definitely do it. I know you can because I did it with depression as well as with anxiety. There is nothing more satisfying than looking back later on and realizing how far you have come. You will look back and think: "How on earth did I think that?" or "Did I really say that to myself?" or "Did I really believe that?" Trust me, you will think these things. You may even laugh out loud at some of the things you used to think when you are sitting on the bus or train or in your car and people might look at you strange and think you have lost it. But the funny thing is you will actually have found it. You will have found your smile; the real you that is full of positive thoughts, optimism and trust. This can only lead to success in whatever it is you want to do with your life.

So remember this statement:

The price you must pay for the success you achieve in changing your mind, is to be eternally vigilant as the gate keeper of your thoughts, your beliefs, your emotions, and, ultimately, your own happiness.

EPILOGUE — IT'S ALWAYS BEEN YOUR CHOICE

When you really get down to it, it's always been a matter of choice. I am sure that you would prefer to believe that you have no choice with regards to how you feel, what you think about, how your life is going, and what has happened to you. Most people would much rather believe that circumstances out of their control lead to them having certain reactions and that there is simply nothing they can do about it. It is my sincere hope that having read this book you have already begun to see how many choices you actually do have whenever something doesn't go your way or doesn't go according to plan. It's always been your choice whether you simply react to the world and then let your emotions take their course or whether you decide consciously and spiritually how you will react to the events in your life both good and "bad."

There are times, even when life has really dealt you a blow or when things just seem to have gone the wrong way, when you feel depressed or down. It is at these moments, just as you begin to feel the emotion welling up inside you and about to spill into you, that you have a choice. You can choose to follow the train of thought that you are upsetting yourself with or you can choose to let the thoughts go and focus your attention on the here and now. Any time we are down, demotivated, or unhappy we have been on automatic pilot and our thoughts have been given free reign to wreak havoc in our minds and our bodies. You have abdicated power and decided that it is too much for you to deal with. You feel that you have no control over your emotional life and that there is nothing you can do but ruminate. Think again. You always have a choice. It may not seem true but when you are just about to go into the thoughts and the emotion is at its starting point, stop, realize what you are doing and decide whether you want to feel sad, depressed or just plain horrible today. Do you? Do you really feel like feeling miserable or would you rather enjoy your day with what you have at your disposal? With the people you *do* have in your life, with the possessions you *do* have to enjoy, with the food you *do* have in your fridge, with the bed you *do* have to sleep in — stop and realize that you are focusing on the negative or lack instead of what's good and abundant in your life. If you or I only focus on all the things that are against us, we will build them up in our minds to a degree that is unwarranted by the facts of our reality. Any time you focus only on what you don't want, what you don't have and what is not right with your world you will no doubt end up feeling really depressed.

The choice you have is what you focus on, how you focus on it and how much importance you give to anything in your reality. If you believe that you cannot enjoy your life without someone special and that you cannot be happy unless you are wealthy, then you are setting yourself up for disappointment if those things don't show up in your life exactly when you wanted them to. You have to choose the beliefs, the thoughts and the emotional states that are going to support you and make you feel good about yourself and your life. I have offered you some tools and techniques in this book to help you get started in changing your mind and thus changing your life. I firmly believe in the power of these techniques to help you overcome any negative emotions, thoughts and situations in your life. Your life can be substantially different than it is now but that doesn't necessarily mean anything would have changed in your external world. You may still be living in an apartment or house that is not ideal, you may still be without the money you wanted, but *you* will be amazingly different because you will feel good about yourself and about life in general. And when you have achieved that first step to freedom — freedom of mind, freedom of thought, freedom of emotional choice and freedom of internal peace —you are well on your way to changing the material or external circumstances of your life.

I challenge you to use the tools and techniques in this book on a *consistent* basis and to still feel exactly the same way after a month or two about your life or any area that was concerning you. There is much more magic and wonder in this world than we dare to believe in sometimes. It was easier when we were kids but it doesn't have to be harder as we grow older — as long as our minds do not grow old. We have to keep our thinking fresh, look out for new and better ways to live and that also begins with a choice.

Some people become very cynical about the world purely because of how they have interpreted the events in their lives; from what they choose to see in the form of evidence for their faulty and irrational beliefs. I used to be friends with a lady who never seemed able to find the right man. She would complain bitterly how all men were jerks or that there just weren't any decent men around, but the problem was that this wasn't the only thing she complained about. She complained about everything and I could just imagine how the men who dated her felt when they went on their first outing together. The negativity that kept pouring out of her and the subsequent endless stream of negative events that kept happening to her were reinforcing each other. At the time I could not offer her formal counselling and I am not sure whether she would have wanted it from me anyway, but I could clearly see that she needed to change her mind, and fast. She needed to make some crucial choices about how she saw her world and how she interpreted everything that happened to her. She needed to realize that she was actively taking part in the creation of her reality and that if she just stopped, changed her mind and created some new beliefs her life would have changed very quickly.

We need to be aware of the times in our lives when we have the choice to choose the path of happiness or the path of sadness and destruction of our emotional lives. It's always been our choice, its one of the greatest gifts that God gave us.

*Victor Frankl wrote about the men who in the Nazi concentration camps had everything they cared about taken away from them: Their family, their friends, their possessions, and everything that had given their lives meaning and comfort. He explained that he saw with his own eyes the real choices that people make and he realised that it ultimately comes down to only one thing; that we have been given the ultimate secret weapon that we can choose to use whenever we want. And that is our power of **choice**. We choose what we focus on, we choose what something will mean to us, we choose which direction we want to go in and most important of all, we choose how we are going to react to what happens to us in our lives. No matter the material or "objective" realities we have going on in our lives we always have a choice. We can choose to see the positive side of things, to laugh and see life as a great big challenge and adventure or we can choose to see it as miserable, dangerous and dark. What is your choice? Will you change your life?*

ABOUT THE AUTHOR

D avid Fox is a registered psychologist with a master's degree in psychology. In studying the principles and counselling approaches mentioned in this book over the past fifteen years and applying them to his own life, he has managed to rid himself of a disorder called GAD (generalised anxiety disorder). In January 2000, just as he was completing his master's thesis, David suffered from a panic attack and subsequently went into a depression for a few months. This painful experience helped him gain some real insight into what people go through when in a depressive state and he thus knows what works and how to achieve long-term recovery from both depression and anxiety. By using the tools and techniques outlined in this book, David managed to lift himself out of fear and anxiety and achieve some great successes, including becoming a black belt in tae kwon do and becoming a registered psychologist both in South Africa and Australia. He understands the power of goal setting, commitment and discipline and the principles in motivating yourself to take action. He has helped people with anxiety disorders, depression, low self-esteem, and those who just found themselves lost in life and needing some coaching and guidance to take their next step forward.

In addition to working as a psychologist, David has worked in the field of human resources for several years while further developing his ideas and tools for positive change. He has counselled managers, staff, and private clients over this time and has always enjoyed helping people take action and find a new meaning in their lives. He sees amazing changes in people when they use the tools described in this book.

David's interest in writing began at 14 when he wrote a compelling short story about two police detectives, set in Los Angeles. He lives in Sydney with his two boys, Jake and Brandon.

David welcomes any feedback you have on this book and material. He can be contacted at <u>david@foxpsychology.com.au</u>

APPENDIX

The Thought Journal

Date/Time	How am I feeling?	What am I thinking?	What could the underlying belief be?	What can I do to change it?

The Thought Worksheet
Just add in as many rows as you need.

Date	Trigger Event or Thought	Automatic Negative Thoughts	Emotional Reaction	Physical Reaction	Label	Alternative Rational Thoughts	% belief	
22.10.09	Sent off a few e-mails to some possible leads	People ignore my e-mails, which means they not interested in working with me	Despondent Frustrated Angry Resentful	Tension in my face — especially in the jaw area	Mind Reading	I cannot tell what people are thinking when they see an e-mail from me. They may receive 100 e-mails a day and find it hard to respond. If I change my mode of communication to over the phone I may prove to myself that it's not about me but how they like to work with people.	60%	

23413657R00091